Th Campsies
and the
Kilpatrick Hills
40 favourite walks

The author and publisher have made every effort to ensure that the information in this publication is accurate, and accept no responsibility whatsoever for any loss, injury or inconvenience experienced by any person or persons whilst using this book.

published by
pocket mountains ltd
The Old Church, Annanside,
Moffat DG10 9HB

ISBN: 978-1-907025-860

Text and photography copyright © Douglas Milne 2022

The right of Douglas Milne to be identified as the Author of this work has been asserted by him in accordance with the Copyright, Designs and Patents Act 1988

A catalogue record for this book is available from the British Library

Contains Ordnance Survey data © Crown copyright and database 2022 supported by out of copyright mapping 1945-1961

Printed by J Thomson Colour Printers, Glasgow

MIX
Paper | Supporting
responsible forestry
FSC® C023105

Introduction

The Campsie Fells, along with the Kilpatrick, Kilsyth, Fintry and Gargunnock Hills, form a sprawling upland range which stretches eastwards from Dumbarton, passing to the north of the city of Glasgow and across the narrow waist of Scotland towards Stirling. The Campsies take their name from one of the hills in the range, Campsie, meaning 'Crooked Hill' and originating from the Gaelic *cam*, 'crooked', and *sith*, 'seat'. The name first appeared on General Roy's map of the area in 1755.

Originally only referring to the mass of hills between the valleys of the Blane, the Forth and the Kelvin, the Campsie Fells have since become synonymous with the entire range of hills between Strathblane and Stirling. Stretching west from Strathblane are the Kilpatrick Hills, named after the village of Old Kilpatrick (from the Gaelic *Cille Phàdraig*, meaning 'Patrick's Church'), which lies at their southern foot. Combined, the Kilpatricks and the Campsies are known collectively as the Lennox Hills.

Glasgow is one of the easiest cities to get away from, and the Campsies and the Kilpatrick Hills, a few short miles north of the city, are the first port of call. This range, it is said, represents Scotland in miniature. Everything that a visitor would expect to find in Scotland – picturesque hills and lochs, medieval castles, warrior clans and whisky – can be found in the Campsies and the Kilpatricks.

This guide covers all of the major hills within both ranges, as well as low-level walks around and between the villages which lie on their perimeters. Many of the walks make use of the West Highland Way and the John Muir Way, which cut through the heart of this area.

History

The Campsies and the Kilpatrick Hills have been populated for millennia. There are Neolithic and Bronze Age cairns at Baldernock, Cochno and Duntocher, and the remains of an Iron Age fort can be found at Meikle Reive, above Lennoxtown. The names of Dumgoyne, Dumfoyn, Dungoil, Dunmore, Duncolm, Dumbuck and Dunbowie mark the historic locations of further hillforts.

The Romans came and went, leaving the Antonine Wall behind them, stretching across the narrowest part of Great Britain between the Forth and the Clyde. By medieval times, stronger defences were needed and the castles of Dumbarton, Dunglass, Mugdock, Bardowie and Culcreuch were built. Fermtouns or clachans began to spring up. These were groups of small dwellings, home to tenant farmers. If the parish church was built at the fermtoun, it became a kirktoun. Surviving kirktouns include Balfron, Fintry and Clachan of Campsie.

Drove roads criss-crossed the landscape, established by drovers travelling to the cattle markets at Drymen and Falkirk. One of these was upgraded to a Military Road following the Jacobite uprisings. Villages as we know them today, such as Buchlyvie and Gargunnock, began to evolve along the Military Road, providing travellers with such services as cobblers, tailors, blacksmiths and bakers.

As the Industrial Revolution took hold, water-powered cottonmills were set up at Balfron and Fintry, and calico printing works were established at Balfron, Strathpie, Lennoxtown and Milton of Campsie. The old drove roads, including the Crow Road and the turnpike road between Fintry and Balfron, were upgraded to service these industries, and the Forth & Clyde Canal, mirroring the route of the Antonine Wall, was built to take the factory goods to Glasgow and onwards across the world.

The natural environment

The Campsies and the Kilpatrick Hills form a broken line of rugged upland and steep, south-facing slopes which stretch from Dumbarton on the Clyde right across Scotland to Stirling on the Forth.

These hills were formed by volcanic intrusion over beds of mudstone, sandstone and limestone, now known as the Clyde Plateau Lava Formation. Dumgoyne and its neighbour Dumfoyn, which dominate Strathblane, are the remains of these volcanoes, as is Dumbarton Rock, at the foot of the Kilpatricks. Some 300 million years ago, a faultline developed north of what is now Glasgow, causing the land to sink and creating the steep southern escarpment. The hills were subsequently scoured out by glaciers moving from west to east across the landscape.

Walkers will find themselves in a rich and diverse range of habitats here. Although there are few natural lochs in the area, several man-made reservoirs and the two major rivers – the Endrick and the Carron – contain Atlantic salmon, brown trout and lampreys, as well as otters and water vole. Blanket bog and upland heath pepper the hilltop plateaux, providing a home to invertebrates such as cranefly, which in turn are food for game birds such as black grouse and grey partridge. Look out for kestrel, hovering over the countryside before swooping down on their prey. Other bird species present are oystercatcher, curlew, lapwing, redshank, snipe, barn owl, short-eared owl, swift, sand martin, skylark, ring ouzel, song thrush, spotted flycatcher, raven, linnet, bullfinch, yellowhammer and reed bunting. Broadleaf natural woodland and conifer plantations extend up the glens and into the hills, offering shelter to red squirrel and pine marten. Deer can also be seen throughout the year.

Public transport

There are regular bus services, mostly from Glasgow or Stirling, to the start of many of these walks. Access by train is more limited, with all services running from Glasgow Queen Street. There is a railway station at Milngavie, which may be used, via the West Highland Way, to access most of the walks in Strathblane. There are also railway stations at Kilpatrick, Dumbarton East and Alexandria, which provide access to the Kilpatrick Hills. The railway station at Croy provides access to Kilsyth, while Lennoxtown and Clachan of Campsie may be reached via a short bus ride from the station at Lenzie.

How to use this guide

This guide contains 40 low-level and hillwalks. The low-level walks are on good paths and tracks, and are generally waymarked or are easy to follow.

For the hillwalks, you should always carry a map and compass and know how to use them. The requisite OS Explorer maps (mostly 348 and OL38, with one route each for 342 and 366) are noted in the text. A whistle and a head torch are also advisable for hill routes, along with a few fully charged USB power packs, spare provisions and a first aid kit, just in case. In winter, be prepared for shortened daylight hours, and for the challenges of poor weather at any time of year.

Walking conditions can change; wet weather can quickly turn an unsurfaced footpath into a quagmire, and steeper slopes can become slippery with mud. Strong winds too, particularly on higher ground, can be dangerous. Many walkers use Global Positioning Systems (GPS), but signals can be lost, and phones can run out of power. GPS can tell you where you are but cannot tell you where to go next in conditions of poor visibility.

Preparation for your walk begins at home. Choose a route that reflects your ability and that of those who will accompany you. Dress appropriately for the weather and the terrain: carrying warm, waterproof clothing is generally advisable, even if you don't use it.

Access

The Land Reform (Scotland) Act of 2003 gives members of the public a right to access most Scottish land and inland waters, and landowners have a responsibility not to unreasonably prevent or deter access. However, key to the Act is that members of the public exercise their rights responsibly, as laid out in the Scottish Outdoor Access Code (www.outdooraccess-scotland.scot).

Take your litter home with you. Respect the environment and private property, and do not damage fences and crops. Close all gates behind you. Dogs should be kept under strict control, particularly in the spring and early summer when they could disturb ground-nesting birds. Do not enter a field with your dog if there are lambs, calves or other young farm animals. If cattle become aggressive, keep calm, let your dog go and take the shortest safest route out of the field.

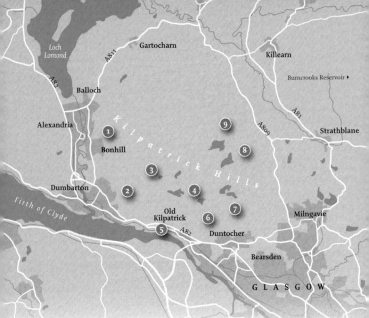

The Kilpatricks, a range of hills with distinct, if low, summits and fine views, stretch from Dumbarton and the Vale of Leven in the west to Strathblane in the east. Many paths and tracks criss-cross the terrain, which is mostly grassy moorland, and walking is generally straightforward.

Strathblane, a broad valley, divides the Kilpatricks from the Campsies. To the north, the hills in the range extend as far as Loch Lomond. To the south, they are separated from the River Clyde by the small towns of Bowling, Clydebank and Old Kilpatrick, which gives its name to the hills above it and is one of several places thought to be the birthplace of St Patrick.

This area was home to the ancient tribe of the Damnonii, and later became part of the Kingdom of Strathclyde. Several of the hills have a history as ancient hillforts (from the Gaelic *dùn*, meaning 'fort'), with names such as Dumbuck, Dunbowie and the highest point in the Kilpatricks, Duncolm, 'Hillfort of St Columba'.

The area also features several reservoirs, including Scotland's oldest, Kilmannan Reservoir. Once you are up in the hills, look out for red deer, otters and osprey.

Most of the towns around the Kilpatricks are served by both rail and road, with the A82 leading up their western edge. And yet you need only be a short distance into the hills for them to feel as remote as any Highland glen.

The Kilpatrick Hills

The Pappert Well Track

Distance 7.9km **Time** 2 hours
Terrain hill tracks, some very damp
underfoot **Map** OS Explorer OL38
Access regular buses and trains to
Alexandria from Glasgow

This route from Bonhill up to the
Pappert Well has been a popular walk
for generations. It began as a drove
road, crossing the Kilpatrick Hills to
Strathblane and following the route
of today's A891/A803 to the market at
Falkirk. The road passes the Pappert Well,
a small natural spring. This circular route
leaves the old drove road to climb
to the summit of Pappert Hill with its
breathtaking views of Loch Lomond
and the Vale of Leven.

The walk begins at the railway station
in Alexandria. Leaving the car park, cross
the road and turn right. Pass St Mary's
Primary School, joining the blocked -off
end of Bank Street. At the far end of Bank
Street, turn left to cross the River Leven.

This arched bridge is the third to cross
the river here. The first, known as the
Bawbee Bridge after the Scottish term for
a halfpenny (the price of the toll), was
built in 1836, but was replaced with a steel-
arched bridge in 1898. Following safety
concerns, that bridge was replaced with
the present structure in 1986.

Beyond the bridge, cross the road
and turn right to walk uphill, crossing
Burn Street, and turning up a flight of
steps 150m or so later. Continue round to
the left, climbing uphill for 400m, before
taking the path on the left signposted for
Pappert Hill and dropping to cross a burn.
This meanders gently through a deep
gorge beside the path, which rises
through woodland, becoming less
distinct as you emerge onto open hillside
and over an old stile.

◀ The Pappert Well

Step over the burn before continuing gradually upwards across a hillside clad with heather, gorse and bracken. In the spring, bog asphodel, tormentil, grass of parnassus, corn spurrey, redshanks and common spotted orchids can be seen on the moorland here, along with butterflies such as small coppers, ringlets and meadow browns.

Bear left, heading towards a broad firebreak between conifers, which quickly narrows to enclose the path. You soon arrive at a damp clearing where a semi-circular wall encloses the Pappert Well. A small informal wooden footbridge leads over a burn to the well. At one time, a ladle by the well made drinking its waters much easier for drovers and local walkers.

Returning to cross the footbridge again,

turn uphill along the right of the burn, shortly emerging from the trees to briefly skirt the woodland's perimeter, before swinging towards the trig point at the summit of Pappert Hill.

From here, Loch Lomond looms large in the foreground, stretching out into the Highlands. The Luss Hills and Arrochar Alps are on the western shore, opposite the huge mass of Ben Lomond. To the west, the River Clyde flows past distant Greenock. The views only improve as you continue along the wide ridge of the summit.

Descend gradually, hopping over a narrow burn before turning right at a junction. Step across another burn to rejoin the outward route. Turn downhill and follow the track back to the start.

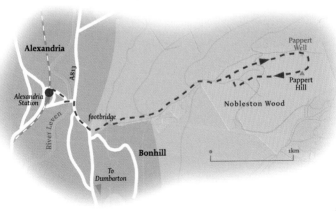

The Overtoun Estate

Distance 3.8km **Time** 1 hour
Terrain woodland tracks, some steep
ascents **Map** OS Explorer OL38
Access buses from Glasgow stop in
Dumbarton, 3km from the start

There are several waymarked walks
around the grounds of Overtoun House.
The estate is a haven for wildlife – look
out for otters, pine martens, ravens,
owls and woodpeckers.

This circuit follows the Overtoun Burn
through a picturesque wooded glen,
before exploring the estate on paths laid
out by Lady Overtoun in the 1860s.

Overtoun House was built in the
Scottish Baronial style in 1862 by the
industrialist James White of Rutherglen.
White had made his fortune after
becoming a partner in the family chemical
firm in 1851, and he bought Overtoun
Farm eight years later, demolishing it to
build his mansion which was designed by

Glasgow architect James Smith. The
house was gifted to the people of
Dumbarton in 1938, and subsequently
became a maternity hospital.

Today, the house holds a Christian
Centre for Hope and Healing, offering
youth activities and accommodation for
women. It has occasionally been used as a
movie location, appearing in the 1997 film
Regeneration and the 2012 film *Cloud Atlas*.

Beginning in front of the house, follow
the road towards Overtoun Bridge,
turning downhill just before reaching it.

The track follows the Overtoun Burn,
which tumbles over the Spardie Linn
waterfalls in the glen deep below, before
crossing it at a bridge. Climb up the other
side, passing paths that loop off to the
side where you can view the waterfalls.
The falls were mentioned by name in a
1609 charter by James VI.

At a yellow waymarker, walk uphill to
cross another bridge, veering uphill again

Black
Wood

◄ Overtoun House

Overtoun Burn

Garshake
Reservoir

Lang Craigs
Wood

Lang
Craigs

0   500m

Overtoun
House

To
Dumbarton

Spardie
Linn

at the fork to arrive at a road. Climb back towards the house but, just before reaching Overtoun Bridge, follow the orange waymarker into the woods to head upstream along the burn. Cross the burn at a bridge, passing a large wooden sculpture of a fish by a pond, and head around the pond, bearing left and following the orange waymarkers through the trees to cross a little stone bridge.

Some of this woodland dates from the original landscaping of the estate in the 1860s, while the Woodland Trust has planted some 234,000 native trees since 2012, including oak, birch, hazel, aspen and Scots pine.

After a short flight of steps, bear right and slope down to cross the burn yet again. Snake back uphill on the other side,

emerging from the trees through a gate in a deer fence out onto the open hillside.

Press on uphill for a little, before turning along the hillside at a waymarker. Climb uphill again at a bench by a tree, crossing another track and meandering around to walk beneath the towering Lang Craigs. These dramatic cliffs were gouged out of a 360 million-year-old lava flow by ice age glaciers, and contain evidence of prehistoric human habitation.

Head downhill again at a junction, passing the conical Welcome Cairn, created by the Woodland Trust after it acquired Lang Craigs Woodland in 2011.

Go through another deer fence and follow the wide road down through the trees to a narrow metal gate at the bottom of the hill, turning back towards the house to finish the walk.

Doughnot Hill

Distance 8.3km **Time** 2 hours 15
Terrain hill tracks, some damp underfoot;
some steep climbs **Map** OS Explorer OL38
Access buses from Glasgow stop in
Dumbarton, 3km from the start

**It is not a long climb to reach the
summit of Doughnot Hill, but it feels
deliciously remote and offers a
magnificent panorama.**

Although it is known locally as The
Doughnut, the similarity between the
name of Doughnot Hill and the sugary
snack is entirely accidental. Like other
hills in the Kilpatricks (Duncolm,
Dumbuck, Dunbowie), it probably had a
hillfort on its summit at one time. It is
named on Pont and Blaeu's 1654 *Atlas of
Scotland* as 'Douennet Hil', and it was

historically pronounced as *Deochnay*.

From the Overtoun House car park, head
towards the house, but immediately turn
uphill through a gate, following the
Craigs Circular Path (signposted) through
the woodland. Beyond another gate, turn
uphill at a conical sculpture with carvings
of leaves and animals. The sculpture,
called the Welcome Cairn, was created by
the Woodland Trust after it acquired Lang
Craigs Woodland in 2011.

Turn right at a junction to follow a
track, which shortly becomes grassy, to
a set of steps that climb up the hillside.
As you gain height, the views to the south
and the west open up over Dumbarton
Rock and Overtoun House, and down the
Clyde, past Greenock towards the hills of
the Cowal Peninsula.

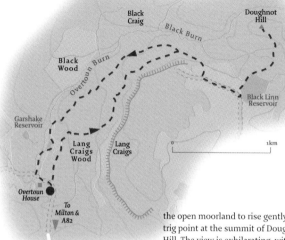

Crossing a grassy knoll where a bench marks a viewpoint, forge ahead beneath the towering Lang Craigs, a dramatic 360-million-year-old line of volcanic cliffs.

Turn right beyond an old drystane dyke to follow a deer fence, turning right at a crosspaths. Reaching a three-way junction 500m further on, keep going straight ahead. Doughnot Hill is directly ahead of you across the valley.

Press on through a gate in the deer fence, turning uphill at a sign for the Craigs Circular Path to reach an aggregate vehicle track. Follow the track downhill, dropping down at a junction to cross the dam of the Black Linn Reservoir. Step over the outlet at the far end and go through the kissing gate beside it.

From here, the grassy track curls across the open moorland to rise gently to the trig point at the summit of Doughnot Hill. The view is exhilarating, with a vista that stretches from the Lang Craigs, the Clyde and the Cowal Peninsula to Loch Lomond and the hills of the Southern Highlands. The Campsies can be seen to the east.

Retrace your steps to the three-way junction, bearing right to follow the track back down the hill.

Reaching a surfaced path, turn right to meander down the hill, passing through a gate and dropping down to a bridge over the Overtoun Burn. The path continues along the burn, climbing away briefly before dropping back down by a short flight of steps to cross back over. Cross again at a bridge beside a pond and a large wooden sculpture of a fish, and press on down the path to arrive at a road.

Cross Overtoun Bridge to return to the car park.

◂ Looking across Lang Craigs from the summit of Doughnot Hill

Duncolm

Distance 14.2km **Time** 3 hours 45
Terrain vehicle track; hill tracks, some
damp underfoot; steep ascents
Map OS Explorer OL38 **Access** buses and
trains to Old Kilpatrick from Glasgow

**This climb from almost sea level to
conquer the three highest peaks in the
Kilpatrick Hills is long but
unchallenging. The first half of the route
is on a vehicle access track, while the
remainder is on a well-defined
unsurfaced footpath.**

Duncolm, Fynloch Hill and Middle
Duncolm are the three highest peaks in
the Kilpatricks, and it is worth leaving this
outing for a clear day to enjoy the
excellent panoramas that they offer.

Leaving the Kilpatrick Hills car park,
across a bridge from Mount Pleasant
Drive in Old Kilpatrick, pass beneath the
Great Western Road (A82) and walk along
the road as it swings to the left. Turn
uphill at a sign for Loch Humphrey to
follow a wide vehicle track up the
Kilpatrick Braes.

The climb is gentle and even, but
relentless nevertheless. The views across
the Erskine Bridge and back along the
Clyde to Glasgow, as well as west to the
Cowal Peninsula, are an excellent excuse
to pause regularly for a breather.

Rounding a shoulder of the hill, the
climb becomes more gradual, meandering
along the hillside for a little before
dropping down to Loch Humphrey. Here,
the steep-sided, flat-topped summits of
Fynloch Hill and Middle Duncolm can be
seen on the horizon.

Carry on beneath Loch Humphrey's
dam, bearing left and passing a small
picturesque lagoon. The road that you

Lily Loch

Duncolm

Fyn Loch

Middle Duncolm

Fynloch Hill

Little Duncolm

Berry Bank

Loch Humphrey

Greenside Reservoir

Hill of Dun

0   1km

Kilpatrick Hills

To Dumbarton

A82

Mount Pleasant

River Clyde

A814

Old Kilpatrick

To Glasgow

have been following since the start of the walk now gives way to a wide, well-worn footpath, boggy in places, which continues over a large stile in a deer fence and up the slope ahead.

At the top of the slope, bear left and traverse the boggy hillside before striding up a brief incline to the summit of Fynloch Hill. This is the finest vantage point on the route. From here, the view over Fyn Loch immediately below the hill, straight down Loch Lomond and into the Southern Highlands is superb.

Turn around and walk back down the hill, turning onto a narrow track that leaves the main track to cut across the heather towards Middle Duncolm. After rejoining the footpath, divert to the right to scramble up Middle Duncolm's short but steep slope before crossing the flat summit and carefully making your way down the bank on the far side.

Hop over the burn at the bottom, and almost immediately begin to climb again, taking the path to the left which winds diagonally up the steep slopes of Duncolm to arrive at the trig point at the summit. As well as being the highest point in the Kilpatricks, Duncolm is also the only Marilyn in the range. It takes its name from the Gaelic *Dun Choluim*,

meaning 'Hillfort of (Saint) Columba'. Columba was a patron of St Patrick, who gave his name to the whole range.

The wider view is similar to that from Fynloch Hill. Lily Loch sits to the northeast, while Greenside Reservoir and the adjoined Cochno Loch and Jaw Reservoir can be seen to the southeast.

Return to Old Kilpatrick by retracing your steps down the hill and following the footpath, bypassing Middle Duncolm and Fynloch Hill.

The Saltings and Bowling Harbour

Distance **4.5km** Time **1 hour 15**
Terrain **flat, mostly surfaced footpaths**
Map **OS Explorer OL38** Access **buses and
trains to Old Kilpatrick from Glasgow**

**This short circuit around a man-made
nature reserve and along to the western
end of the Forth & Clyde Canal is packed
with history.**

The Erskine Bridge dominates most of
the route. Built in the late 1960s and
opened in 1971, the bridge replaced a ferry
service across the Clyde which had run
since 1777, when the river was dredged to
allow for larger ships. The crossing was
originally established in the 1700s when,
at low tide, it was possible to walk across
the Clyde from Old Kilpatrick to Erskine
on the opposite bank.

The route begins at The Saltings car
park, which can be accessed from
Dumbarton Road by crossing the bridge

across the Forth & Clyde Canal onto
Erskine Ferry Road.

From the car park, take the path through
the gate, beneath the Erskine Bridge and
across the Dalnottar Burn. Bear left at the
crosspaths, staying on the main path to
curve around the nature reserve, enjoying
occasional views across the Clyde. At one
time, this area was saltmarsh which
became flooded whenever the river,
swollen with rainfall, met with high tide.

When the Erskine Bridge was
constructed, spoil was dumped on the
saltmarsh, raising the soil level. The spoil
has since been reclaimed by nature. Look
out for wild orchids, peacock and orange-
tip butterflies, common blue damselflies,
common hawk dragonflies and birds such
as cormorant, swan, heron, curlew and
oystercatcher.

Bear left again at another crosspaths to
skirt around a metal barrier. Turn away

◀ Bowling Canal Basin

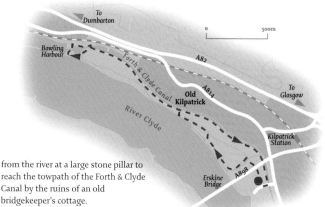

from the river at a large stone pillar to reach the towpath of the Forth & Clyde Canal by the ruins of an old bridgekeeper's cottage.

The bridgekeeper would have been responsible for the Ferrydyke Bascule Bridge. The westernmost fort of the Antonine Wall originally stood on the opposite bank from here. The Forth & Clyde Canal parallels its route across Scotland to Bo'ness on the River Forth – two massive engineering projects built almost two millennia apart.

Continue past the bridge. In just under 1km, the far side of the canal becomes crowded with barges and narrowboats.

Drop down to pass beneath an old railway viaduct, built in 1896 to carry the Caledonian and Dunbartonshire Railway across the canal. After the railway closed in 1960, the viaduct fell into disrepair, but it has been restored and the arches converted into retail units.

Go through a gate on the other side of the bridge to arrive at Bowling Canal Basin, where boats large and small are berthed. Circle around the basin. At the far end, beyond the basin, the decaying hulks of abandoned boats can be seen nestling in the mud at Bowling Harbour at low tide.

Pass beneath the railway bridge again and cross back to the towpath, following it all the way back along the canal to Erskine Ferry Road. Here, the Old Kilpatrick Swing Bridge crosses the canal. Built in 1935 by Sir William Arrol and Company, it formerly carried traffic down to the Erskine Ferry.

Turn right, then right again into The Saltings, passing a carved totem pole to return to the car park.

The Slacks

Distance 8.1km **Time** 2 hours 15
Terrain unsurfaced hill tracks; steep
ascent and descent **Maps** OS Explorer 342
and OL38 **Access** buses and trains to Old
Kilpatrick from Glasgow

The steep escarpment of The Slacks
looms above the village of Old Kilpatrick.
It looks daunting, but the well-worn
track up to the summit is a relatively easy
climb and this is a popular route with
Glaswegians looking for a day out in
their local hills.

Leave the Kilpatrick Hills car park, across
a bridge from Mount Pleasant Drive in Old
Kilpatrick. Head back down the hill and
beneath the A82. Stay on the pavement
until it runs out, then go through the gate
into a field on the next corner.

Follow the grassy track across the field
and up the steep lower slopes of The

Slacks. Go through another couple of
gates before zigzagging up to a waterfall.

Pass through another gate and bear left
beyond a stile, admiring the excellent
views across Glasgow and along the Clyde
towards Inverclyde.

This area is known as Feuar's Muir, a
'feuar' being the landowner. In 1851, Lord
Blantyre, who co-owned the land with
Robert Lang of Allteth and Miss Agnes
Colquhoun Jaffray, wanted to divide it
into plots rather than keep it for open
grazing. But the plots he devised
surrounded Lang and Jaffray's plots with
his own and left them with no access to
running water. Lang and Jaffray argued
that this rendered their plots impractical
for grazing purposes. The dispute was
finally settled in 1857, when it was agreed
that rather than fence off the plots, the
boundaries were to be marked with 12

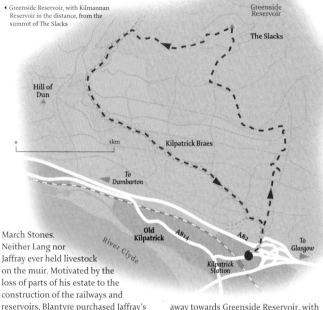

◄ Greenside Reservoir, with Kilmannan Reservoir in the distance, from the summit of The Slacks

March Stones. Neither Lang nor Jaffray ever held livestock on the muir. Motivated by the loss of parts of his estate to the construction of the railways and reservoirs, Blantyre purchased Jaffray's plot in 1863, and Lang's 10 years later. One of the March Stones, inscribed with the letters B, J and L, sits beside the track.

On meeting another path, turn uphill, continuing straight ahead at a junction. The Slacks gets its name from the Old Norse word *slakki*, these being the 'shallow valleys' that run between the drumlins littering the broad summit of the hill.

From the trig point, which sits on the highest drumlin, the wide expanse of Loch Humphrey can be seen to the northwest, with the rounded summit of Duncolm straight ahead. The hill drops away towards Greenside Reservoir, with Kilmannan Reservoir beyond.

To continue, walk westwards along the shallow ridge of the drumlin, dropping to meet with an old fence. Swing northwest at the corner of the fence, following it to meet with a wide vehicle track.

Turn left to follow the vehicle track across a shoulder of the hill, before striding easily downhill, enjoying the expansive view along the Clyde to the Erskine Bridge and onwards to Glasgow. Reaching a junction at the bottom of the hill, turn left and follow the road back to the beginning of the walk.

Jaw Reservoir and Cochno Hill

Distance **12.8km** Time **3 hours 15**
Terrain **surfaced and unsurfaced tracks,
some damp underfoot; several short
steep ascents** Map **OS Explorer OL38**
Access **buses to Faifley from Glasgow**

**The route from Faifley to the summit
of Cochno Hill is a well-trodden one.
This longer alternative circuit crosses Jaw
Reservoir to approach the hill from the
north. For the shorter (7km, 2 hours)
route, continue uphill at the fork
beyond the dam to head straight for
the summit. Look out for the remains
of several shielings scattered around the
route, where subsistence farmers would
bring their animals for summer grazing.**

The route begins at the car park for
Auchnacraig Woodland Park, in Faifley.
From the car park , turn right, shortly
leaving the road to carry on uphill,
following the signs for Jaw Reservoir.

After turning right through a kissing
gate, continue along the side of a field

and through two more gates to follow a
wide track between two fences. Go
through another gate at the far end and
continue up the hill, following the line of
a burn which is variously known as the
Jaw Burn or the Cochno Burn.

Pass the Grey Mare's Tail waterfall
to reach the dam of the Jaw Reservoir.
The Jaw Reservoir, impounded by an
earth embankment dam, was opened in
1887. It is also known as the Edinbarnet
Reservoir. Near the far end of the dam is
a 'Starfish' control bunker built during
the Second World War. Decoy fires would
be lit here, and in other places around
the hills, in order to confuse Luftwaffe
bombers. Unfortunately the raids were so
widespread that the decoy fires did little
to avert the Clydebank Blitz of March 1941.

Bear left past the dam to briefly
continue climbing, but head downhill at a
fork to follow the reservoir shore past the
remains of an old corrugated-iron
boathouse and across the causeway that

◄ The old boathouse
  beside Jaw Reservoir

separates Jaw Reservoir from Cochno Loch. The latter is a natural loch, but the water level was artificially raised in the 19th century.

At the far side, turn left, following the shore for a little before climbing away from the loch and turning left onto a forest vehicle track. Stroll gently uphill along the track, bearing left by a quarry. As the track curves, Dumgoyne and Dumfoyn can be seen across Strathblane.

Reaching a junction above Kilmannan Reservoir, take the minor vehicle track to the left which climbs through conifers, now heading southwest. The vehicle track peters out at an old drystane dyke but continues uphill as a muddy track, swinging around to pass through a deer gate before rising steeply. Cochno Loch and Jaw Reservoir can be seen again across the hillside.

Pass between two gateposts with no gate or fence attached, and climb the hill beyond, swinging back towards Cochno Loch again. Beyond a deer gate, begin climbing Cochno Hill, turning right at a crosspaths and right again at the next junction to arrive at the summit.

From here, Clydebank, Bearsden and Glasgow stretch out below. Tinto Hill can be seen on the southern horizon and

Ailsa Craig to the southwest. To the southeast, the Pentlands can be seen on the horizon, and Ben Lomond and the Trossachs to the north.

Forge straight ahead across the summit and down the other side, turning towards Glasgow and descending to meet a surfaced path. Continue downhill on the path, going through a gate at the bottom to join a minor road. Reaching a junction, turn left and follow the road back to the car park.

Burncrooks Reservoir

Distance 12.8km **Time** 3 hours 15
Terrain surfaced tracks, some gentle
slopes **Maps** OS Explorer 348 and OL38
Access no public transport to the start

**Beginning at an historic former inn
immortalised by Sir Walter Scott, follow
the John Muir Way into the Kilpatrick
Hills, alongside one reservoir and
circumnavigating a second.**

This is a new section of the Way,
completed in 2016 at a cost of around
£500,000 as part of the Central Scotland
Green Network project, an ongoing
initiative to develop and promote
Scotland's environmental credentials.
Although part of the work upgraded 2km
of existing track, the rest was built from
scratch, using a helicopter to bring in
three bridges and bags of materials to
build the path.

The walk begins at a large lay-by on the
A809, opposite the St Mocha Coffee Shop,
beside the historic Carbeth Inn. The inn
was more than 200 years old when it
closed in 2015. Sir Walter Scott called it a
'miserable hovel' in his 1817 novel *Rob Roy*.
Much later, it featured several times in the
television detective programme *Taggart*.

A roadside path leads south from the
lay-by. When you reach the road to the
Auchineden Estate, turn right along it,
briefly following the John Muir Way
before bearing left, passing gorse, broom

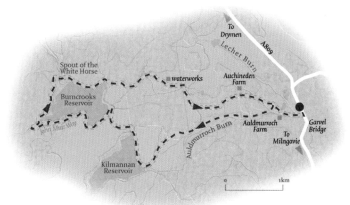

and, in summertime, wild raspberries.

After 1.7km, fork gently up the hill to the right, alongside a conifer plantation. Stay on the main track at the next junction to arrive shortly at Kilmannan Reservoir. Built in 1775, it has the distinction of being the oldest artificial reservoir in Scotland. The shapely peak of Duncolm can be seen across the water.

Walk along the reservoir shore, before climbing away from it to pass a quarry, bearing right after this to stay on the main track. Rejoin the John Muir Way, following the waymarks around the Burncrooks Reservoir, which you reach almost immediately. The 51ha reservoir was completed in 1915. It is a popular fishing spot, and is stocked with brown and rainbow trout.

From here the view is stunning, looking straight down the distant valley of Loch Lomond, with the Arrochar Alps and the Luss Hills on the left and the towering summit of Ben Lomond on the right. Closer to hand, the distinctive shard of The Whangie can be seen on the hillside above the reservoir.

The track meanders around the water before climbing to pass through a deer fence and dropping to cross a bridge over the Burn Crooks, which feeds the reservoir. Drop down to pass in front of the dam before turning uphill again to climb to a fishing car park, and continuing along the edge of the reservoir. Go through a deer gate, following the reservoir's access road through another gate and past its water treatment plant.

Carry on downhill to a junction, turning right to follow the John Muir Way back to the outward route, where you retrace your steps to the start.

The Whangie

Distance 4.5km **Time** 1 hour 15
Terrain well-defined hillside path, damp
underfoot in places **Map** OS Explorer OL38
Access no public transport to the start

Local folklore says that The Whangie,
a huge slab of basalt that has become
detached from Auchineden Hill, is the
work of the Devil. After hosting a
gathering of witches and warlocks in
the Kilpatrick Hills, he is said to have
been flying to another such meeting.
As he crossed Auchineden Hill, he
flicked his tail, wrenching apart the
hillside below.

In truth, this striking geological feature
on the northern edge of the Kilpatrick
Hills was caused by a geological
phenomenon called glacial plucking.

During the last ice age, Scotland was
covered in huge glaciers that carved out
the lochs and the Highlands. Here,
the extreme cold froze a glacier to the
hillside. As the glacier began to move,
it took the rock with it, causing a long
fracture to appear.

The route begins at the Queen's View
car park, just off the A809. It is so named
because this spot gave Queen Victoria her
first view of Loch Lomond when she
visited the area in 1879. A path from the
car park leads to a stone stile over a
drystane dyke, beyond which a series of
duckboards cross a small boggy area.

Follow a wide grassy track, passing
through a gate in a deer fence and rising
to a rocky outcrop. This vantage point
gives great views of Ben Lomond and the

◄ The entrance to The Whangie

Arrochar Alps, as well as Loch Lomond.

A few metres further on, by a drystane dyke, leave the path to take a track up the hill, climbing quite steeply at first before levelling out to follow the path westwards across the wide, flat ridge of Auchineden Hill. There are several tracks here, but all ultimately converge at the trig point at the western end of the hill.

Continue westwards from the summit to drop down a slope, turning left at the bottom to swing around the foot of the hill and arrive at a fork. Going right takes you into the mysterious hidden pathway known as The Whangie. Whangie is Scots for 'slice' – for example, 'a whang o'cheese' – and The Whangie does indeed look as if somebody has sliced into the

mountain, leaving a chasm around 100m long, 1m wide and 9m deep. A minor scramble is required to enter, but it is an easy, if claustrophobic, passage.

Alternatively, going left at the fork takes you through various jagged stones and rocky outcrops. These pinnacles were rendered from the rock by the movement of the glacier. Both paths converge again at the northern end beyond a prominent pinnacle known as The Gendarme.

Continue across the lower slopes of Auchineden Hill, which can be extremely boggy, before rising to head east below the hill's northern escarpment, eventually joining the outward route and following it back to the car park.

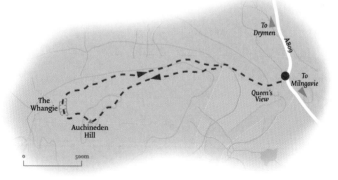

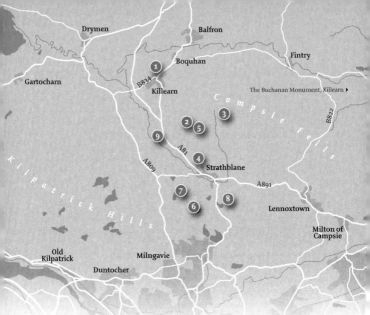

The Buchanan Monument, Killearn ▶

Strathblane (from the Gaelic *Strath Bhlàthain* – 'the Valley of the Blane', after the river that runs through it) separates the Kilpatrick Hills from the Campsies.

This broad valley is dominated by the volcanic plug of Dumgoyne – its distinctive rounded summit can be seen from most of the routes in this chapter. The first stage of the West Highland Way leaves Milngavie to pass along the edge of Mugdock Country Park before traversing the length of Strathblane and continuing towards Loch Lomond and the Trossachs.

Mugdock, which sits to the south of Strathblane, is thought to have been the location of a battle between the Picts and the Britons of Strathclyde in 750AD, in which Talorgan mac Fergusa, brother of the Pictish king Óengus I, was killed.

The principal family in Strathblane were the Edmonstones of Duntreath, descended from King Robert III, whose family seat, Duntreath Castle, sits near the tree-covered hill, Dumgoyach.

One more recent resident of the castle was Alice Frederica Edmonstone (*aka* Alice Keppel), mistress to Edward VII.

The Blane Valley Railway ran near Duntreath Castle, and the Edmonstones had a private halt erected on the line so that the King could quietly disembark from the Royal train for discreet liaisons. Alice's great-granddaughter is Camilla, Queen Consort.

Mugdock and Strathblane

Killearn and the Endrick Water

Distance 7.9km **Time** 2 hours
Terrain country roads and unsurfaced
riverside tracks **Map** OS Explorer 348
Access regular buses to Killearn from
Stirling and Glasgow

**This peaceful walk leaves Killearn to trace
a route through the countryside before
following the Endrick Water back to the
start. The Endrick lies on a popular drove
route through the Carron Valley from
Drymen. Indeed, its name is thought to
derive from the Old Celtic word *anderik*,
meaning 'heifer'.**

Beginning at Killearn Village Hall on
Balfron Road, cross Station Road and
head out of the village, following the
footpath by the A875 for 1.5km.

Where the B818 to Fintry forks off on
the right, veer downhill on the minor road
to Balfron Station. After 500m or so, head
along the signed public path to Boquhan,

which is lined with oak and beech trees.
This is Jenny Gunn's Loan. The daughter
of a veteran of the Napoleonic Wars, Janet
Gunn, known as Jenny, was born in
Boquhan in 1821. She lived in her father's
home in Boquhan until her death in 1904.

Beyond the village, rejoin the A875 and
follow it downhill. Just before the Endrick
Water, take the wide tree-lined vehicle
track that leads off along the riverbank.

Rising in the Fintry Hills, the Endrick
Water is formed from the confluence of
the Burnfoot and the Backside Burns. It
flows south from the hills before veering
westwards near the western dam of the
Carron Valley Reservoir. From there, it
flows through Strathendrick, passing
Fintry, Balfron and Drymen before
entering the southeastern corner of
Loch Lomond. The river is teeming with
wildlife – look out for kingfisher,
oystercatchers and redshanks.

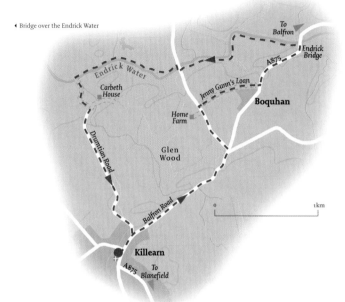

◄ Bridge over the Endrick Water

Reaching a field, a narrow track continues along the riverside, quickly becoming a pleasant woodland amble.

Soon after crossing a burn, a couple of bridges come into view. After going through an old metal gate beneath the modern roadbridge and the stone archway of the older bridge, climb up to cross the old bridge. As part of the scheme to provide Glasgow with fresh drinking water from Loch Katrine, this bridge was built in 1864 to carry both the pipe and a road across the Endrick Water. There are staircases providing access to the pipe at either end. The pipe burst in the 1990s and the bridge was replaced by the modern roadbridge next to it.

Drop back down to the river on the other side of the bridge, meandering along the bank to reach a wide, deep burn. Divert briefly upstream to cross at a small metal footbridge before returning to the river. Cross a stile, presently arriving at a wooden footbridge across the river.

Cross the bridge and walk uphill away from the water, bearing right onto Drumtian Road and following it back into Killearn.

Dumgoyne

Distance 7.5km **Time** 2 hours
Terrain wide surfaced vehicle track; rough
hillside tracks with some very steep
inclines **Map** OS Explorer 348
Access buses to Glengoyne Distillery
from Stirling and Glasgow

This pleasant walk avoids the well-worn
tourist path to the top, which goes
straight up from Glengoyne Distillery, in
favour of a longer and more circuitous
route. Dumgoyne is the most popular
hill in the Campsies, and its distinctive
rounded summit dominates Strathblane.
The 427m-high hill is a volcanic plug –
the remains of the hardened lava of a
volcano after the softer cone has been
worn away by glacial erosion.

Head up the private road opposite a
lay-by a few metres north of Glengoyne
Distillery. Bear right to go through an

ornate gateway and over an old stone
bridge which crosses the Glengoyne Burn
as it tumbles down to feed the distillery
below. Walk on uphill through the trees,
emerging through a gate by a large house
onto an open pasture.

Dumgoyne looms above, but merge
with another track, continuing south
across the field. This is the maintenance
track for the 19th-century Glasgow
Corporation Water Works scheme to pipe
water from Loch Katrine to Glasgow.

Continue along the track, enjoying
views along Strathblane to the rounded
tree-covered lump of Dumgoyach,
another volcanic plug. Go straight over
a crossroads, turning uphill at the next
junction before swinging towards the
hillside and crossing a burn by an
old bridge.

Almost immediately beyond the bridge,

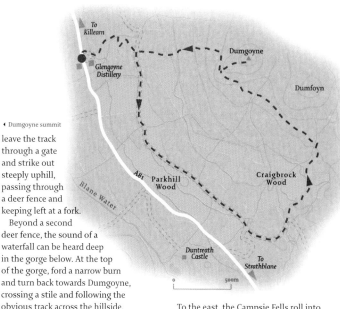

◀ Dumgoyne summit

leave the track through a gate and strike out steeply uphill, passing through a deer fence and keeping left at a fork.

Beyond a second deer fence, the sound of a waterfall can be heard deep in the gorge below. At the top of the gorge, ford a narrow burn and turn back towards Dumgoyne, crossing a stile and following the obvious track across the hillside.

Distant Loch Lomond, in the shadow of the Luss Hills, comes into view as you traverse the lower slopes of Dumfoyn, the hill to the south of Dumgoyne.

Bear right beyond another burn to continue towards Dumgoyne. By a large boulder, the track begins to climb very steeply up the hill. Reaching a junction, continue up the well-worn path to the summit. Here, an upright stone which once sported a metal view indicator was helicoptered into placed and erected by the Strathendrick Rotarians in May 2000. The 360-degree view is superb but keep well away from the edge.

To the east, the Campsie Fells roll into the distance. To the north, Conic Hill, Ben Lomond, and the islands of Loch Lomond can be seen. Meanwhile, in the south the wooded Dumgoyach is in the foreground, with Strathblane stretching out towards the distant Carbeth and Craigallian Lochs and onwards to Glasgow.

Having enjoyed the summit views, turn around and head back down again, forging straight ahead at the junction where you joined the track.

Reaching the bottom of the hill, cross a double stile and bear right to follow the outward route back to the beginning of the walk.

Earl's Seat

Distance 10.4km **Time** 3 hours
Terrain well-defined but initially very
steep hill path, very damp underfoot in
places **Map** OS Explorer 348 **Access** regular
bus to Glengoyne Distillery from Stirling
and Glasgow

At 578m, Earl's Seat is the highest
point in the Campsies. Its name refers
to the Earldom of Lennox, which held
the lands around the southern end of
Loch Lomond between Dumbarton
and Kilsyth. This walk, though initially
a challenging climb, soon levels out,
quickly becoming a gentle hilltop
stroll with some of the best views in
Lowland Scotland.

Head up the private road opposite a
lay-by a few metres north of Glengoyne

Distillery. Bear right to go through an
ornate gateway and over an old stone
bridge which crosses the Glengoyne Burn.
Walk on uphill through the trees,
emerging through a gate by a large house
onto an open pasture. Continue uphill,
crossing another track and heading
directly for the shapely round prominence
of Dumgoyne.

Cross two stiles in quick succession,
then bear left to wind up the very steep
and uncompromising slope, heading left
again by a large rock to skirt around the
side of Dumgoyne, where the path quickly
levels out.

Bear left again, hopping across a
shallow ditch, and slowly begin to climb,
leaving Dumgoyne behind you.

Beyond the shattered remains of an old

◀ Cairn on Ballagan Tops

shieling on the slopes of the wonderfully named Clachertyfarlie Knowes, climb to a small cairn on the summit of Garloch Hill. From here, Killearn can be seen below, with the distinctive obelisk of the Buchanan Monument rising from the middle of the village. Loch Lomond stretches into the distance beyond.

Dropping down from Garloch Hill, step over a low fence and climb gradually, crossing Bell Craig to reach a large cairn on Ballagan Tops. The cairn commands superb views across Balfron and Buchlyvie towards the Lake of Menteith and the Trossachs.

Stride out eastwards from the cairn towards the trig point on the summit of Earl's Seat, crossing a fence just before reaching it. Located on an undulating plateau, the summit is far less distinctive than Dumgoyne or Meikle Bin, which sits prominently on the eastern horizon, with the radar station on Holehead below it. Stronend and Carleatheran can be seen to the north.

The trig point sits beside a fence, which marks the border between Stirlingshire and East Dunbartonshire.

Take the obvious, very straight track that leads away from the trig point across the heather-clad moorland back towards Garloch Hill. Care should be taken here, as the track peters out in places amid peat hags and can be very wet underfoot.

Meeting up with the outward track just below Garloch Hill, walk back down the hill to return to the start point.

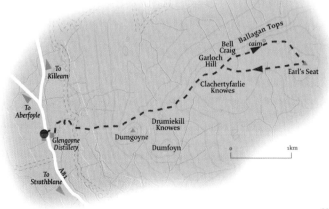

The Pipe Track

Distance 8.9km **Time** 2 hours 15 (one way)
Terrain mostly good surfaced track
Map OS Explorer 348 **Access** buses to
Blanefield and Killearn from Glasgow
and Stirling

**This route offers tantalising views down
the whole of Strathblane to the distant
Arrochar Alps, while the volcanic plugs of
Dumgoyach, Dumgoyne and Dumfoyn
dominate the early stages.**

During the Industrial Revolution in the
first half of the 19th century, Glasgow
grew rapidly. Cholera epidemics in 1832,
1848 and 1853 highlighted a pressing need
for fresh unpolluted water. Loch Katrine,
in the Trossachs, was chosen as the
source, and work began on a subterranean
aqueduct in 1855. It was inaugurated by
Queen Victoria in 1859.

As the city continued to expand, an
additional supply was needed and a
second aqueduct, following the same
route, was opened in 1901. The aqueducts
are still in use today. While they are
mostly underground, a number of
masonry bridges carry the pipes across
the many narrow gorges that score the
hillside here.

This straightforward walk between the
villages of Blanefield and Killearn follows
a road that was built to service the
aqueducts by the Glasgow Corporation
Water Department around 1885. It begins
at Blanefield's war memorial, following
Campsie Dene Road to its end and
continuing straight ahead through the
woodland beyond.

The small square building above the
path is a valve house where the flow of
water in the aqueduct was controlled.
A cylindrical shaft nearby contains a
junction chamber, allowing the water to
be diverted along either or both of the
two aqueducts. You will encounter several
more of these shafts along the route.

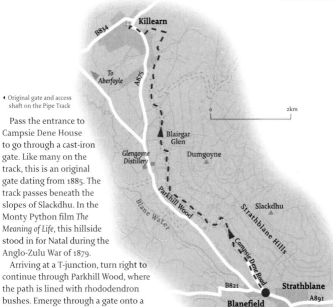

◄ Original gate and access shaft on the Pipe Track

Pass the entrance to Campsie Dene House to go through a cast-iron gate. Like many on the track, this is an original gate dating from 1885. The track passes beneath the slopes of Slackdhu. In the Monty Python film *The Meaning of Life*, this hillside stood in for Natal during the Anglo-Zulu War of 1879.

Arriving at a T-junction, turn right to continue through Parkhill Wood, where the path is lined with rhododendron bushes. Emerge through a gate onto a large open field beneath the slopes of Dumgoyne. At the far side, bear right again to enter more woodland, dropping down to cross Blairgar Glen by a footbridge. Leaving the trees, cross another field. The track peters out at a gate, but continue along a raised grassy ridge. Pass to the rear of some houses and through another gate. The track, which leads through Kirkhouse Wood, quickly arrives at a junction. Swing down a long narrow road, turning downhill again at the end to drop down to Killearn's Main Street. Turn right to finish the route at the huge obelisk of the Buchanan Monument.

Born in Killearn in 1506, George Buchanan was a historian and humanist. He was tutor to both Mary Queen of Scots and her son, James VI, and served as one of the earliest Moderators of the General Assembly of the Church of Scotland. His writings formed the basis for the Scottish Reformation and were influential on the formation of the American constitution.

Retrace your steps to Blanefield. Alternatively, for a circular walk, you can follow the line of the Blane Valley Railway.

Dumgoyne and Dumfoyn

Distance **5.7km** Time **2 hours**
Terrain **grassy but very steep path,
muddy in damp weather**
Map **OS Explorer 348** Access **regular buses
to Glengoyne Distillery from Stirling
and Glasgow**

Dumgoyne is probably the best loved
hill in the Campsies, but most complete
the long slog to the summit only to
turn around and traipse back to the
bottom of the hill again. This route
extends the walk with an easy stroll to
Dumgoyne's twin, Dumfoyn, a little
to the east.

Both hills are volcanic plugs, the
remains of the hardened lava of a volcano
after the softer cone has been worn away

(in this case by glacial erosion during the
ice ages). However, be warned: the slopes
of Dumgoyne are steep and it is hard
going at times. Take your time, stop
regularly for a breather and to enjoy the
magnificent views that gradually open up
around you, and remember that there is a
distillery at the bottom of the hill; a well-
deserved reward for getting to the top.

Beginning in the lay-by on the A81,
opposite and slightly north of the
Glengoyne Distillery, cross the road and
cut around the right-hand side of the
distillery. Walk over the field to cross a
stile. Follow the track steeply up the hill,
crossing another track, and over two more
stiles only a metre or so apart. Keep right
where the path splits. Although it starts

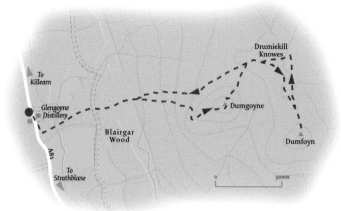

as a gradual climb, the ascent becomes very steep very quickly.

Eventually, the path bears right, and the going becomes gentler. It curves around a false summit and almost immediately reaches the top, which is marked with an upright stone, helicoptered into placed and erected by the Strathendrick Rotarians in May 2000. At one time, a metal view indicator was attached to the stone, but this has been removed.

The view is superb. Conic Hill, Ben Lomond and the islands of Loch Lomond can be seen to the northwest. To the south the heavily wooded Dumgoyach is in the foreground, and further in the distance, Carbeth and Craigallian Lochs. Glasgow stretches off into the distance. To the west, the Kilpatrick Hills stand sentinel over Strathblane.

Continue straight over the summit to make your way carefully down the very steep path on the other side.

Keep straight ahead, turning right at a crosspaths to curl around a hillock and start to climb steadily uphill.

Look out for a narrow grassy track which undulates across the hillside towards Dumfoyn. The huge, narrow bulk of Dumfoyn is at its most impressive from here, and the steep slopes on the northern and southern sides make you wonder how you ever got to the summit.

Jump over the beginnings of a stream, climbing again briefly before heading across a gently sloping plateau. As the track begins to slope upwards, it joins an ATV track to make the final ascent towards the summit.

Return the way you came, ignoring the grassy track to follow the ATV track across the plateau and eventually meet up with a well-defined track. Turn downhill, and follow the track around the side of Dumgoyne and back down to the beginning of the walk.

◀ Dumgoyne and Dumfoyn from the West Highland Way

Mugdock Country Park

Distance 3.8km **Time** 1 hour
Terrain surfaced track throughout; some
mild inclines **Map** OS Explorer 348
Access the nearest buses and trains stop
at Milngavie, 4.5km from Mugdock
Country Park on the West Highland Way

**Mugdock Country Park was at one time
the estate of the Barony of Mugdock, and
was home to the Graham clan from the
mid-13th century.**

The lands were purchased from the Earl
of Lennox by David de Graham of Dundaff
in the mid-13th century. Mugdock Castle
was built by his descendants in the 14th
century. The Grahams remained at
Mugdock Castle until 1682, when they
bought Buchanan Auld House, near
Drymen. The castle fell into ruin
thereafter. Parts of it were demolished in
the 19th century by the antiquarian John
Guthrie Smith, who built himself a

Scottish Baronial house among the ruins.

Smith's house was subsequently
purchased by Hugh Fraser, owner of the
House of Fraser retail chain, but was
destroyed by fire in 1966. The estate was
gifted by Fraser's son to Central Regional
Council in 1981 for use as a country park.

Beginning at the visitor centre, take the
path signed for Craigend Pond downhill
past the Victorian Walled Garden,
originally built by the owner of Craigend
Castle to provide food for the estate.

Continue around the pond, turning left
at a crosspaths to wander across a grassy
meadow, keeping to the main path to
descend to a junction. Turn left towards
Mugdock Loch.

Follow the signs for Mugdock Castle to
circumnavigate the loch, climbing
gradually on the southern shore. Stroll
past the front of Mugdock Castle, walking
through a gate and along a tree-lined

◀ Mugdock Castle

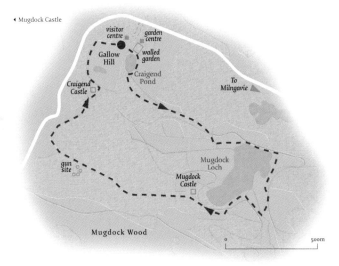

drive across open parkland towards the Khyber Car Park. The Kilpatrick Hills can be seen straight ahead. The remains of a Second World War anti-aircraft gun site flank the path. Erected in 1942 following the Clydebank Blitz, it formed part of the Clyde Basin anti-aircraft defence.

Beyond another gate, by the car park, turn downhill, following the signs for the visitor centre and bearing left to follow a wire fence around the rear of derelict Craigend Castle. Built by James Smith of Jordanhill in 1816, in its heyday Craigend Castle was the height of opulence, boasting oak panelling, carved stone ceilings and silk wallpaper. It was bought

by Andrew Wilson, owner of Wilson's Zoo in Glasgow, who transformed the surrounding estate into Craigend Zoo in 1949. The zoo's main attraction was Charlie the Elephant, who lived in the former stable block – now the visitor centre. One day, Charlie's keeper went for a drink in Milngavie, but was unaware that he was being followed. The elephant got itself stuck in the pub doorway and had to be freed by the fire brigade. Despite Charlie's escapades, the zoo operated at a loss and closed in 1955.

At the next junction, head uphill to return to the visitor centre and the start of the walk.

The Craigallian Fire

Distance 8.6km **Time** 2 hours 15
Terrain surfaced and unsurfaced tracks;
some mild inclines **Map** OS Explorer 348
Access the nearest buses and trains stop
at Milngavie, 4.5km from Mugdock
Country Park on the West Highland Way

The Craigallian Fire was a significant
piece of 20th-century walking history.
Situated on the slopes above Craigallian
Loch, it became well known during the
1920s and '30s as an informal meeting
place for walkers, climbers and many
impoverished and unemployed people
seeking to escape the Great Depression
in Glasgow and the Clyde.

Here, they would chat, socialise and
even sleep, before heading along what is
now the West Highland Way to Loch
Lomond, or following the Loch Katrine
aqueduct onwards into the Trossachs.
They gathered around a campfire which

was said to have burned continuously
from around 1920 until the outbreak of
the Second World War, when it was
extinguished for fear that it would guide
enemy bombers.

Beginning at Mugdock Country Park
Visitor Centre, head past the playpark.
Take the middle path at a three-way fork
to go down the hill. Turn to cross a bridge
over the remains of the old Craigend Zoo
paddling pool, now reclaimed by nature.

Beyond the bridge, climb through
woodland, turning left down Craigallian
Road at the top.

Go through a wooden gate signposted
for Cuilt Brae Road to continue through
the woodland. Turn downhill again at
another road, and then left towards the
West Highland Way. Ford a burn and,
beyond a gate, turn left onto the Way
itself. The Way passes the Carbeth Huts.
The Carbeth Hutting Community started

◄ Site of the Craigallian Fire

in the aftermath of the First World War, when ex-servicemen began to build holiday shacks in the forest, with the support of the Craigallian Estate. Numbers peaked in 1941, when refugees of the Clydebank Blitz set up their homes here. Workers would trek daily across the Kilpatrick Hills to the shipyards at Clydebank, while their children were schooled at Blanefield. Today, the land is owned by the Carbeth Hutters Community Company, who lease the land to the hutters.

Continue along the West Highland Way. As Craigallian Loch comes into view, look out for a memorial to the Craigallian Fire. The memorial marks the birthplace of Scotland's outdoors movement. Many of those who sat around the fire would become influential writers or outdoor educators and go on to campaign for greater access to Scotland's countryside.

Leaving the loch behind, continue along the banks of the Allander Water, bearing right to cross some duckboards and eventually arrive at a road. Head uphill and go through a metal gate.

Continue on the West Highland Way, passing into woodland and bearing left to leave the Way behind as you follow the signs for Mugdock Castle.

Cross the duckboards, climb some steps and bear right to cross a couple of little bridges. Climb uphill again through a stone gateway to emerge from the trees and head across an open pasture towards Mugdock Castle.

Take the path downhill to the left of the castle to cross some more duckboards and follow the signs back to the visitor centre.

41

Loch Ardinning Wildlife Reserve

Distance 4.1km **Time** 1 hour 15
Terrain good, well-defined paths,
though damp underfoot on the muir
Map OS Explorer 348 **Access** no public
transport to the start

Loch Ardinning was formed at the end
of the last ice age, when meltwater
collected in hollows carved out by
glaciers. Although it is a natural loch,
the water level was raised in 1796 by
building a small dam in its northwest
corner to supply power to the mills of
Strathblane. Today, the Scottish Wildlife
Trust manages the loch and the
surrounding areas of wetland, woodland,
grassland and moorland.

The route begins in a lay-by just off the
A81, by a sign for the Scottish Wildlife
Trust Loch Ardinning Wildlife Reserve,
around 4km north of Milngavie.

The path parallels the road for a little,
before turning into the reserve itself at
another sign. Cross a bridge and pass a
quarry, which was the source of the stone
for the A81 when it was originally built in
the early 19th century. Ignore the path
which leads off up the hill, and bear left
at the next two forks. In spring and early
summer, the woodland here is carpeted
with bluebells and wood sage. Where the
soil is thinner, plants such as heather and
blaeberry thrive.

Keep left again to leave the woodland at

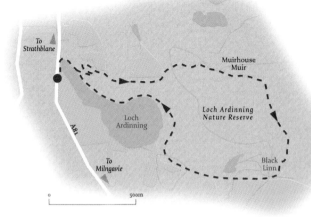

a gate, and climb a short set of stone steps by an old wall to reach a bench. There are superb views across Strathblane to Dumgoyne and Dumfoyn, with Ben Lomond and the Arrochar Alps in the distance. From here, the route crosses Muirhouse Muir, initially offering views along the southern edge of the Campsies.

A huge rock known as Catcraig, meaning 'Battle rock', marks when Gwallag King of Cumbria defeated Hussa, son of the King of Bernicia, at the Battle of Ardunnion in around 570AD.

At the top of a slope swing sharply right, passing scattered rocks to reach a large cairn at the summit of Muirhouse Muir. During the Second World War, this was the location of a civil lighting decoy site. Fire baskets mimicked fires caused by bombing raids, in an attempt to draw the Luftwaffe away from industries in Glasgow and Clydebank.

Beyond the cairn, the route becomes very damp underfoot, as it drops downhill to enter a small wood. Turn sharply right by a waterfall to walk beside a burn, crossing it by a wooden walkway.

Emerging from the trees, follow an old drystane dyke to wind down the hill towards Loch Ardinning, traversing above the shore before swinging west through a gate and back into the Wildlife Reserve.

The Scots pines here were planted many years ago, but are now allowed to seed naturally. Crossbills can sometimes be seen feeding on the seeds from the pinecones. Trees on the reserve are allowed to regenerate naturally, and examples of young Scots pine, willow, rowan and birch can be seen here.

As the path rises along the lochside, look out for the ridges and furrows of the distinctive runrigs of 18th-century small-scale agriculture.

Joining the outward route, return to the beginning of the walk.

The Blane Valley Railway

Distance 11km **Time** 2 hours 45 (one way)
Terrain obvious, rough-surfaced track
throughout, with several modest climbs
and descents **Map** OS Explorer 348
Access regular buses to Killearn and
Blanefield from Glasgow and Stirling

**This historic route traces the West
Highland Way along the former Blane
Valley Railway.**

The railway carried passengers from
Killearn Station to Glasgow. The route, an
extension of the Campsie Branch Line
which ran between Glasgow and
Lennoxtown, opened in November 1866.
Originally intended as a tourist line to
Inversnaid via Aberfoyle, capital could not
be raised and it only ran as far as Killearn,
mostly carrying milk into Glasgow. An
1882 extension took the railway as far as
Aberfoyle, but it remained underutilised.

One prominent passenger was King
Edward VII, who took the Royal Train
along the line to visit his mistress, Alice
Keppel, at Duntreath Castle. Despite a
brief reprieve during the Second World
War, when regular munitions trains
travelled between Aberfoyle and Glasgow,
the railway closed in 1959.

The route begins beneath the Buchanan
Monument in Killearn. Walk briefly
towards the village before turning right
to stroll down the Main Street. At a
roundabout, head downhill on Drumbeg
Loan, taking either fork at the bottom of
the hill to turn left onto the old railway
line, now the waymarked West Highland
Way. After around 200m, the former
trackbed crosses the A81 to reach the
Beech Tree Inn. This popular watering
hole, often the first stop for many walkers
on the West Highland Way, incorporates a

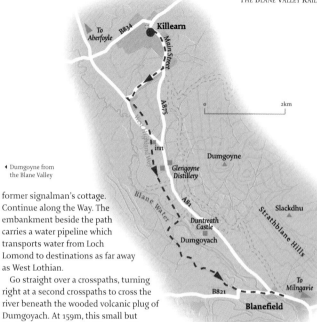

◄ Dumgoyne from
the Blane Valley

former signalman's cottage.
Continue along the Way. The
embankment beside the path
carries a water pipeline which
transports water from Loch
Lomond to destinations as far away
as West Lothian.

Go straight over a crosspaths, turning
right at a second crosspaths to cross the
river beneath the wooded volcanic plug of
Dumgoyach. At 159m, this small but
distinctive hill is dwarfed by its siblings
Dumgoyne and Dumfoyn. Like them, the
outer cone has been eroded away by the
glaciers of the ice ages, leaving only the
hardened lava of the core.

The path swings downhill here,
dropping into the wide, open valley of
Strathblane to pass around the southwest
of the hill. Beyond Dumgoyach, in the
field on the left, are the Duntreath
Standing Stones, which date from the
early or middle Neolithic period. Only
one stone is now upright, and this
aligns with a notch in the hills on the
eastern horizon, which in turn aligns

with the rising sun of the spring and
autumn equinoxes.

Bear left at a fork to leave the West
Highland Way, keeping left to pass
through a gate. Turn uphill, following a
stony vehicle track to meet with a minor
road (the B821). Follow the road down
into Blanefield, turning right onto the
main road through the village to reach
the war memorial and the end of the walk.

Retrace your steps to return to Killearn.
Alternatively, follow the line of the Pipe
Track to complete a circular walk.

The Craw Road, now known as the Crow Road, began as a drove road across the Campsies between Clachan of Campsie and Fintry. Indeed, its very name is derived from the Gaelic word for cattle, *crodh*. To the north, it continued to Drymen. To the south, it went across Blairskaith Muir and onwards into the Borders.

The road was a frequent haunt of Rob Roy and the MacGregors. Rob Roy MacGregor's business interests centred around the weekly cattle market at Drymen, but he augmented his living by demanding 'black rent' or 'black meal' (the source of the word 'blackmail') from the lairds and farmers around the Craw Road. In return, he offered protection from cattle rustlers (his own men).

Later, the route was used to transport coal from the pits of the south to the industries of the Endrick Valley. Coal was carried in hundredweight sacks. Normally,

a horse could be expected to carry three hundredweight of coal, known as a 'load', but the 1 in 6 gradient of the Craw Road was so steep that horses could only carry half a load.

In 1795, Peter Spiers, a Glasgow tobacco merchant, founded the Culcreuch Cotton Mill in Fintry. Around the same time, Robert Dunmore, Laird of Ballindalloch, founded the Ballindalloch Cotton Works further along the Endrick Water in Balfron. Wishing to take advantage of the newly built Forth & Clyde Canal, between them they provided finance for the realigning and regrading of the Craw Road, reducing gradients to a level where wheeled traffic could negotiate it. This allowed them to transport their cotton across the Campsies by horse and cart to Kirkintilloch, where it would be loaded onto barges and taken into Glasgow. In places, the original Craw Road can still be seen above the new Crow Road.

The Crow Road

Dunmore Hillfort

Distance 2.9km **Time** 1 hour 30
Terrain very steep hill track to summit
Map OS Explorer 348 **Access** buses to
Fintry from Balfron and to Balfron from
Glasgow and Stirling

Dunmore Hillfort sits on a rocky
promontory above Fintry. Its layout
– an upper citadel with enclosed areas
below – is typical of the early medieval
period. It is thought to date from around
400-800AD.

The walk begins on the Main Street in
Fintry, opposite the fountain. This was
erected in 1902 to commemorate the
coronation of King Edward VII.

Fintry grew up along the Craw Road
from Culcreuch Castle, built on the lower
slopes of Stronend in 1296 by Maurice
Galbraith. It was the seat of Clan
Galbraith until 1624. It subsequently
passed to the Napier family, of logarithm

fame, who in turn sold it to Alexander
Spiers of Glasgow in 1769. Spiers' son,
Peter, erected a cottonmill and a distillery
in Fintry, and built the modern village to
provide accommodation for his 260
employees on the south side of the main
road. Unfortunately, the mill failed and
had closed by 1864.

Walk up Dunmore Gardens and then
Quarry Road, which rapidly becomes a
gravel track leading up between the
houses and into woodland. Ford the burn
and follow it upstream for a little as it
tumbles down in a series of small
waterfalls. Cross a stile to emerge onto
open hillside, heading along a track at the
foot of the hill before swinging upwards.

Continue up on the main track, which
rapidly becomes very steep, ignoring all
deviations. A little to the west of the track
is a hollow, formed by a rockslide, named
the Covenanters' Hole. A conventicle – an

◄ Dyke on Dunmore route

illegal open-air religious meeting – was held here in May 1679. When soldiers arrived from Stirling to disperse the crowd, a battle commenced. It resulted in the capture of one shepherd boy, who was released shortly afterwards.

The track becomes less steep as it passes through a shallow gorge, where a rockfall has littered the base of the crags with boulders.

Clear the brow of the hill, following a tumbledown drystane dyke between two rocky outcrops, and passing through it at a corner. Curve around the hill, branching off to climb steeply up to a cairn near the summit.

The cairn was constructed out of rocks taken from the debris of the fort. Some of the fort walls were up to 3m thick. Lines of rubble chart their course. There are also circular and rectangular foundations – the remains of shielings and shepherds' huts – which are much more recent than the fort.

Continue past the cairn across the summit plateau to the far end, which is the genuine summit. The panorama from here looks across Strathendrick to Loch Lomond, with the Luss Hills and Arrochar Alps on its western shore. Conic Hill sits in front of it. The Highland Boundary can be followed eastwards until it is obscured by the Ochil Hills. Retrace your steps back down to Fintry.

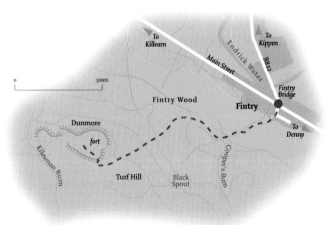

Dungoil

Distance 8km **Time** 2 hours
Terrain surfaced forest road for most of
the route; rough grassy track on the
boggy summit **Map** OS Explorer 348
Access no public transport to the start

**At only 424m, Dungoil is a relatively
small hill, but it offers superb views
across the Carron Valley to the reservoir
and over to the Southern Highlands.**

The majority of this route is along a
vehicle access track. The hill is very steep
on the northern and eastern slopes, but
the track curls beneath these to its gentler
western side, gradually rising to the wide
summit, where the cairn is less than 1km
away from the start.

Begin the climb at the gateway around
3.75km up the Crow Road from Fintry.
When parking, be sure not to block the
gate or otherwise cause an obstruction as
it is in regular use. Parking is limited here.

Climb over the stile beside the gate,
and walk up the hill towards Dungoil,
which looms impressively straight
ahead. After a few hundred metres, go
through another gate to access Dungoil's
lower slopes.

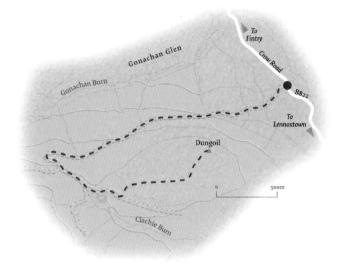

Bear left at a fork, climbing steadily and passing a small quarry before swinging sharply to the left, where the track quickly levels out.

Keep left at the next fork. The summit can be seen, as well as the track snaking up towards it. Bear left again to round a corner, where a rough track soon leads off on the left towards the summit.

After a brief steep climb, the path levels out to wind across the wide, undulating summit of Dungoil, heading for the rounded knoll towards the eastern end of the hill.

Beyond the knoll, continue on to the next hillock, where the path suddenly turns left to cross a series of ridges.

It was long assumed that these were the remains of an ancient hillfort, buried under the soil, but no evidence of any building has been found, and these are now thought to be an entirely natural feature. The summit is marked by a very small cairn and the view is impressive. The beginning of the route can be seen immediately below, with Gartcarron Hill beyond and the Carron Valley Reservoir stretching out to the east.

To the north, the distinctive shape of Stronend is in the immediate foreground, while the Southern Highlands, particularly Ben Lomond and Ben Ledi, line the horizon. Behind you, to the southwest, is the radar station on the summit of Holehead.

There is no way off the hill other than to retrace your steps back to the beginning of the walk.

Holehead

Distance 5.7km **Time** 1 hour 30
Terrain surfaced vehicle track; optional
unsurfaced track to summit
Map OS Explorer 348 **Access** no public
transport to the start

**The walk to the summit of Holehead is
very easy – some might even go so far as
to call it dull – but the reward is a
breathtaking panorama as far north as
the Highlands and as far south as the
Southern Uplands.**

Holehead's name derives from the Scots
hole, meaning 'hollow', in reference to
Campsie Glen below, and *head*, 'a high
place'. The hill's prominence made it an
ideal location for a Met Office Weather
Station. It is part of a network of some 24
such stations and radio sites, along with
more than 200 automatic stations, used
by the Met Office to monitor the UK's
weather systems.

The walk begins at a gate around 4.3km
up the Crow Road from the Campsie Glen
Waterfall car park. There is limited parking
here, so please park considerately. The
gate leads to a rough vehicle track which
stretches up the hill across Campsie Muir.

As the track rises, Dungoil can be seen
to the north and the Southern Highlands
beyond. The distinctive conical summit of
Meikle Bin is directly behind you.

STRATHKELVIN
RAMBLERS 1992

After climbing gradually for around 2km, the weather station comes into view, and the track swings around behind it to approach it from the northwest.

The weather station, a large white ball sitting on the roof of a cabin and surrounded by a high security fence, tracks the weather within a 50km radius. It was built in 2008, replacing a weather station that was situated on Corse Hill, south of Glasgow. Wind turbines have been shown to adversely affect meteorological radio facilities, and the Corse Hill Station was removed due to the installation of the Whitelee Windfarm.

The view from the weather station takes in Stronend, Carleatheran, Meikle Bin and the Carron Valley Reservoir. In the distance, to the northeast, the Ochils escarpment can be seen, with the Lomond Hills beyond.

Completists may want to clamber over the fence and follow the grassy and sometimes boggy track for around 200m to the trig point. The trig has a plaque to the Strathkelvin Ramblers, who adopted it in 1992, and who maintain it.

From the trig point, there are panoramic views across Glasgow and beyond to the Southern Uplands. From the radar station, follow the vehicle track back to the Crow Road.

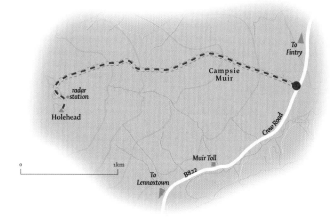

◀ Holehead trig point

Campsie Glen

Distance 2.4km **Time** 45 minutes
Terrain mostly surfaced path, narrow
muddy track down to the Falls of
Alicompen **Map** OS Explorer 348
Access buses to Clachan of Campsie from
Glasgow and Kilsyth

**This short but enjoyable stroll begins
from the square in the pretty hamlet of
Clachan of Campsie and shadows the
Kirk Burn as it tumbles down through
Campsie Glen.**

The route has been popular for more
than 200 years. It was created by the local
landowner, John McFarlan, Laird of
Ballencleroch, in 1785. Known as 'the
Liberal Laird', he opened up Campsie Glen
as an amenity for ordinary working
people. Today, it is notable for giving the

young Tom Weir his first taste of
Scotland's hills, leading to a hugely
influential career as a broadcaster
and hillwalker.

Following the sign for 'Campsie Glen
Walks', go around the building at the
northeastern corner of the square and
onto a narrow path that leads towards
the hills.

Skirt around a gate and bear left at
the junction beyond. Just after the
junction, look for the remains of a
19th-century bleaching works, which
employed 51 people in 1851. Within 30
years it had closed as textile
manufacturing became more mechanised.

Walk alongside the Kirk Burn as it
tumbles over a series of small waterfalls.
There are a number of picturesque picnic

◀ Wee Alicompen waterfall

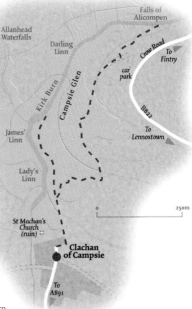

Falls of
Alicompen

Allanhead
Waterfalls

Darling
Linn

Crow Road
To
Fintry

car
park

Campsie Glen

B822

Kirk Burn

James'
Linn

To
Lennoxtown

Lady's
Linn

0   250m

St Machan's
Church
(ruin)

● **Clachan
of Campsie**

To
A891

spots here beneath the mature trees.

Arriving at the end of the path, a large carved wooden hand tells you to stop. The path does go on beyond, but it is quite precarious and has collapsed into the burn in several places. Turn around and return to the junction again, taking the other path to meander up the hill away from the burn.

Views across to the Southern Uplands and Tinto Hill begin to open up as you climb. Numerous paths lead off down towards the glen for views of the waterfalls, but continue up the main path.

Soon, at a sign warning of steep drops, a muddy path leads off through a kissing gate down a set of wooden steps to reach the impressive Falls of Alicompen.

The path reaches the falls at the top of the larger of the two, known as Muckle Alicompen. Its smaller sibling, Wee Alicompen, is straight ahead.

The upper part of the track you left lower down can be seen beside the larger fall, but do not venture down here as some sections have collapsed into the burn and other parts are held up by tree roots alone. Instead, retrace your steps back down to Clachan of Campsie.

Cort-ma Law

Distance 8.7km **Time** 2 hours 15
Terrain well-defined grass track
throughout, initial steep climb; boggy
in places **Map** OS Explorer 348
Access the nearest bus stop is at Clachan
of Campsie, a 1km walk through Campsie
Glen to the start

The huge escarpment of Cort-ma Law
towers over Lennoxtown and Milton of
Campsie. This popular walk begins with
a steep climb but soon levels out,
crossing open moorland and following
the edge of the escarpment to reach the
trig point at the summit.

The route begins at the Campsie Glen
Waterfall car park. Sitting 3km up the
Crow Road from Lennoxtown, at an
altitude of 223m, it is known as the 'Car
Park in the Sky'. The car park has an

excellent view across Glasgow. During the
Second World War, an anti-aircraft battery
was positioned here to protect the city
from approaching German bombers.

From the car park's lower exit, cross the
road and follow the track directly up the
hill, keeping right at the fork to pass an
old, brick-built shelter. It takes some
effort to climb the very steep grassy track,
which can prove slippery in wet weather.

At a crosspaths, cross the remains of the
original Craw Road, the old drovers' road
between Lennoxtown and Fintry.
Continue straight up the hill, ignoring
any of the paths that lead off to the left or
right, to arrive at Crichton's Cairn.

According to one tradition, the cairn is
named after James Crichton, who became
the third minister of the Parish of
Campsie since the Reformation in 1623.

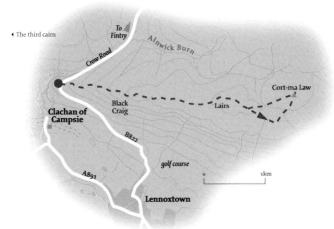

◀ The third cairn

A fit man, Crichton could reach this point from the manse in Clachan of Campsie in 20 minutes, where he would study his sermons. He was deposed in 1629 for 'corrupt doctrine'. Nevertheless, he remained a popular man and when he died his parishioners built the cairn in his memory.

The cairn marks where the climbing stops, and from here you can traverse the wide undulating plateau that climbs gradually to reach a second cairn.

The view behind you takes in the summit of Ben Lomond, peering over Hart Hill directly across Campsie Glen. Looking to the north, the weather station on top of Holehead is visible, as well as the shoulder of Stronend and the distinctive Highland peaks of Ben Ledi and Ben Vorlich.

Continue across the open hillside,

hopping over a low fence to reach the minor summit of Lairs.

Keep right at a fork and cross a narrow burn, aiming for a third cairn in the distance. This cairn offers a fine panorama across Glasgow to the massed turbines of the Whitelee Windfarm beyond. Kilsyth, Kirkintilloch and Cumbernauld are closer at hand. On a clear day, the islands of Arran and Ailsa Craig can be seen in the southwest.

Walk northeast towards the summit of Cort-ma Law, where a trig point is visible on the horizon. Cross a small wooden bridge and climb gently to the top of the hill. From the summit, turn hard left and follow the track across the hilltop, descending slightly to cross a couple of stiles. Follow the track back to join the outward route, and retrace your steps down to the car park.

Fin Glen and the Allanhead ruin

Distance 3.3km **Time** 1 hour
Terrain surfaced vehicle tracks and steep
hill tracks **Map** OS Explorer 348
Access buses to Clachan of Campsie
from Glasgow and Kilsyth

**The Campsies were once notorious for
the number of illicit whisky stills hidden
away in the deep glens, and it was the job
of the local excisemen to keep them
under control. It was said that the route
of Fin Glen could be traced by the smoke
from the seven such stills that were
operating there.**

Clachan of Campsie grew up around the
now ruined 12th-century St Machan's
Church. A number of shops and cafés sit
in front of it, at the back of the village
square. The larger building at the end of
the row is Aldessan House. Built in 1818
as the Crown Inn, it was extremely
popular with visitors to Campsie Glen. In

1922, it became the far more genteel Red
Tub Tearooms. Between 1936 and 1938, a
boxing ring was erected beside the
tearooms, which was used by Benny
Lynch, Scotland's first World
Championship boxer, to prepare for
fights, attracting thousands of visitors.

From the square, take the main road out
of the village. Turn immediately right
along Knowehead Road, beginning to
climb almost straight away. Beyond a gate
the road becomes a rough vehicle track.

After a double bend, turn uphill,
passing a small memorial to the Eritrean
Martyrs. The memorial was placed here in
June 2010 by the Scottish Eritrean
Community. In Eritrea, Martyrs' Day, on
20 June, is celebrated by planting trees,
which watch over children and promote
environmental security. Three trees
planted around the memorial symbolise
the 65,000 Eritreans who died in their

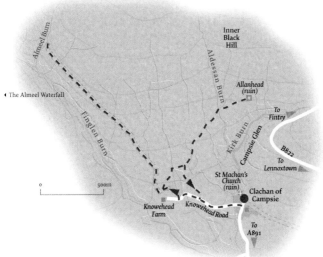

◄ The Almeel Waterfall

Inner Black Hill

Allanhead (ruin)

To Fintry

Campsie Glen

St Machan's Church (ruin)

Clachan of Campsie

To Lennoxtown

Knowehead Road

Knowehead Farm

To A891

0   500m

country's independence campaign.

Skirt around a barrier and walk along the side of Hart Hill. Dumbreck rises on the other side of the glen, with Finglen Burn bubbling far below. Behind you, there is a superb vista back down the glen, across Kirkintilloch, Coatbridge and Airdrie to the Southern Uplands.

After a while, rounding a corner, you arrive at an impressive waterfall, where the Almeel Burn falls into a pool before continuing to drop in a series of smaller waterfalls across the track and down into Finglen Burn.

Having admired the waterfall, return to the barrier and turn uphill to follow a grassy track that leads through a firebreak between conifers. Go through a gateway in an old drystane dyke, ford a burn and

head through another firebreak in the trees. Soon, Campsie Glen Waterfall car park can be seen on the hillside opposite – a reminder that despite the peace and quiet, civilisation is not far away.

Some stepping stones cross another burn. Continue up the hill to reach the ruins of Allanhead Farmstead.

The building is very old, appearing on the maps made by General Roy in the wake of the Battle of Culloden. It is described as a shepherd's house in an 1867 Ordnance Survey reference book.

Turn around and head back down the hill again. Bear left at a fork to follow an old drystane dyke down the hill. Emerge onto Knowehead Road and follow it back into Clachan of Campsie.

Lennox Castle

Distance 6.7km **Time** 1 hour 45
Terrain surfaced paths, woodland tracks
and minor country roads; some mild
ascent **Map** OS Explorer 348
Access buses to Lennoxtown from
Glasgow and Kilsyth

**A pleasant walk on the edge of
Lennoxtown into the grounds
of crumbling Lennox Castle, returning
by a former railway line.**

Lennoxtown, originally known as
Newtown of Campsie, grew up as a factory
town around a calico printing works which
was established here in 1780. By the early
1800s, Charles Macintosh (of waterproof
coat fame) had established an alum works
here. The Edinburgh and Glasgow Railway
built the Campsie Branch Line from Lenzie
to Lennoxtown in 1848 primarily to serve
the printworks, but it also brought
passengers into the town.

Beginning at the junction of Main
Street, Milton Road and Chestnut Walk,
stroll down Chestnut Walk. Cross the
bridge over the Glazert Water, taking the
narrow footpath, second on the right,
signed for Station Road. This track is
known as Lovers' Lane.

The woodland track, which runs
parallel to the Glazert Water, soon widens.
Leaving the woodland, continue straight
ahead along a minor country road.
After 1km, head through a large brick
gateway, formerly the South Gate to
Lennox Castle, and up the Private Road
through the trees.

After a further 500m, skirt around a
barrier to walk uphill. Go around another
barrier at the top of the hill, bearing right
to descend on a road lined with trees and
shrubs. Beyond a gate, the road descends
to arrive at the old stone gateway into the
grounds of Lennox Castle.

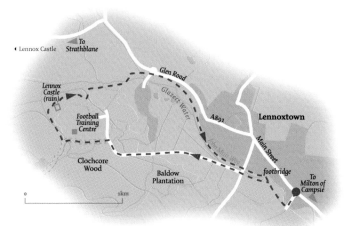

Lennox Castle
To Strathblane
Glen Road
Glazert Water
Lennox Castle (ruin)
Football Training Centre
A891
Lennoxtown
Main Street
Clochcore Wood
Baldow Plantation
footbridge
To Milton of Campsie
0   1km

The castle was completed in 1841 by John Kincaid-Lennox. The family fortune was depleted over the next few generations, and the house and its grounds were sold to the Glasgow Corporation in 1927, who converted it into a Mental Deficiency Hospital. Originally housing both patients and staff, it eventually became the nurses' home. It was closed in 2002, and severely damaged by fire in May 2008.

Wander past the old hospital and down a rough-surfaced tree-lined road. Look out for the remains of Woodhead House, the previous seat of the Kincaid-Lennox family, through the trees to the left. The towerhouse was built by John Lennox, 6th of Balcorrach, around 1572. After the family moved to Lennox Castle, Woodhead House was partially demolished to leave a romantic ruin in the castle grounds.

Walk downhill on the road through the woodland, swinging across the Glazert Water at a bridge and continuing straight ahead through the woods. Meeting with the Strathkelvin Railway Path, turn right.

This is the former trackbed of the Blane Valley Railway, a sleepy Victorian branchline. Completed in the 1860s, it extended the North British Railway's Campsie Branch, which ran from Lenzie to Lennoxtown, through Strathblane and onwards to Aberfoyle.

Arriving at a road, cross over, turning left, then immediately down the path on the other side, marked for the John Muir Way, to return to the Railway Path.

Continue along this, passing beneath a couple of railway bridges. Cross the river again after 1.7km and continue along the path to arrive back at Chestnut Walk.

Turn uphill to return to the beginning of the route.

Mealybrae

Distance 7.1km **Time** 2 hours
Terrain surfaced and unsurfaced tracks;
minor country roads; some mild ascent
Map OS Explorer 348 **Access** the nearest
bus stop is in Lennoxtown, a 3-4km walk
on forest tracks or road to the start

Blairskaith Muir is the location of Lennox
Forest, which covers a large part of the
former moorland, but historically coal,
lime, sandstone and slate were mined at
workings across the muir. The shafts
have long been filled in and now appear
as grassy hillocks.

The walk begins high on Blairskaith
Muir. To get there, turn up Station Road
from Lennoxtown and climb the single-
track road as far as it goes, where there is
a small car park by a barrier.

The road up to the car park from
Lennoxtown is part of the original drove
road known as Mealybrae, which

continued the Crow Road over the South
Braes. The unusual name is from the
Scots word *mealie*, meaning 'oatmeal', and
may refer to the texture of the zeolite
rocks found in the area.

Skirt around the barrier to follow the
wide, rough track across the grassy
hillside, turning downhill at the first
junction. Where the main track swings
left, continue on a narrow unsurfaced
track that leads off down the hill and over
a stile, passing through the less formal
woodland of Peathill Wood. Look out for
wildflowers such as orchids, bird's foot
trefoil, silverweed and ragged robin.

Ford a burn and cross another stile to
descend a poorly drained track. Reaching
a farm road, keep straight on, turning
right onto Tower Road at a crossroads and
then continuing on this to meet a
junction. Turn right to carry on along
Tower Road.

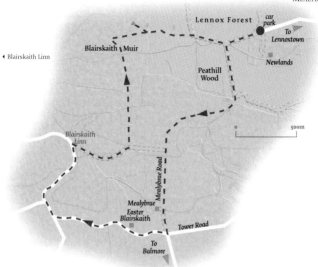

Lennox Forest · car park
To Lennoxtown
Blairskaith Muir
Newlands
◄ Blairskaith Linn
Peathill Wood
Blairskaith Linn
0   500m
Mealybrae Road
Mealybrae Easter Blairskaith
Tower Road
To Balmore

Turn uphill at the next corner, following a single-track road to pass a lay-by, and diverting down a narrow track which drops quite steeply to the burn below.

The waterfall at the end of the track is Blairskaith Linn, which tumbles over the entrance to Linn Caves, an old limestone mine which was worked using the stoop and room method, where 'rooms' of limestone were dug out, leaving pillars, or 'stoops', as roof supports. The mine extends for some distance beyond the sill but, as with all old mine workings, it should not be entered or explored. There was a limekiln on the other side of the burn from here, where the limestone was heated to produce quicklime.

Return to the road and carry on up the hill, turning towards Lennox Forest at the top. Go through a gate, also signposted for Lennox Forest, and carry on up the long straight track beyond. Go through another couple of gates and up the hill, swinging sharply right to run along near the summit of Blairskaith Muir.

To reach the trig point, keep going to the next gate, climb the stile on the left just before it and follow the short track across the moorland. There are excellent views straight down Strathblane towards the Luss Hills and the Arrochar Alps.

Return to the path, go through the gate and walk along the track through the trees towards Lennoxtown. Crossbills love these conifers. Listen out for them in the canopy overhead.

Meeting with the outward route, follow it back to the car park.

The skyline above Kilsyth is dominated by the steep escarpment of the Kilsyth Hills, which rises to heights of well over 300m to a ridge along the summit between Meikle Bin in the west and Tomtain in the east, before dropping down to the Carron Valley beyond.

The ridge was used historically as a drove route, offering hillside grazing for the cattle and avoiding tolls on the roads to the north and south of the Campsies. Drovers ascended the ridge from the Craw Road, or perhaps even climbed into the Campsies from Balfron, Killearn or Strathblane. After heading along the ridge and across the Tak-Ma-Doon Road, the route led down the gentle slopes of the eastern hills and onwards through Denny to the cattle market at Falkirk.

Perhaps the most significant historical event in the area was the Battle of Kilsyth, fought on 15 August 1645, when James Graham, Marquess of Montrose, led a Royalist army to victory over General William Baillie's Covenanters. The battle took place around what is now Banton Loch, an 18th-century reservoir to the east of the Colzium Lennox Estate.

The Kilsyth Hills

Meikle Bin

Distance 10.5km **Time** 3 hours
Terrain surfaced vehicle access track,
steep grassy hill track, damp underfoot
Map OS Explorer 348 **Access** no public
transport to the start

At 570m, Meikle Bin is the highest of the
Kilsyth Hills, and the second highest in
the Campsies. It is 8m lower than Earl's
Seat, but more prominent. Its name
simply means 'Big Hill', and its
distinctive pyramid towers above the rest
of the range from whichever direction
you view it.

 This walk is signposted from the start,
guiding the hundreds of walkers who
climb this popular hill along a forest track
before ascending the bare upper slopes.
The walk begins at the Todholes car park,
on the B818 by the western end of the
Carron Valley Reservoir.

 The reservoir is dammed at both ends.
While the dam at the eastern end allows
the River Carron to escape onwards
towards the Firth of Forth at
Grangemouth, here the dam prevents the
reservoir from affecting the Endrick Water,
which flows westwards towards Loch
Lomond on the opposite side of the road
from the car park. Just under 1km further
west, and signposted from the road, the
Endrick tumbles over the spectacular
Loup of Fintry waterfall, which is well
worth a visit while you are in the area.

 Exit the car park via the gate to head up
a wide surfaced vehicle access track past
the western dam, climbing gradually
before sweeping eastwards above the
reservoir's southern shore. Bear left at the
next two forks before descending gently
to cross a bridge over the River Carron
where it flows into the reservoir.

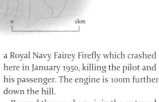

◀ Strathendrick from Meikle Bin

Turn uphill through conifer woodland at the next junction, then bear left and almost immediately right to head uphill between the trees, still following the vehicle track.

Continue up the track for 1km or so before emerging from the woodland beneath the towering pyramid of Meikle Bin. Follow the track along the hillside, climbing steadily.

Rounding a corner, a sign for Meikle Bin points off uphill – take this narrow surfaced footpath as it begins to zigzag up the hill, before quickly disintegrating into a damp grassy track which leads steeply and directly straight up the hill, levelling briefly before continuing its relentless journey towards the summit. Continue straight uphill at a junction to reach the trig point on the small rounded summit.

On a clear day, the views are terrific, from Arthur's Seat and Bass Rock in the east to the hills of Arran in the west, and northwest straight down Strathendrick to the distant Southern Highland peaks.

Turn right at the summit to head back down the hill, passing the wing section of

a Royal Navy Fairey Firefly which crashed here in January 1950, killing the pilot and his passenger. The engine is 100m further down the hill.

Beyond the wreckage, join the outward track and head downhill back to the beginning of the walk.

Your descent will be gentler than that of the mountaineer, William Naismith, who skied from the summit of Meikle Bin in March 1892, in the first recorded instance of skiing in Scotland.

Carron Valley Reservoir Shore Trail

Distance 4.5km **Time** 1 hour 15
Terrain good undulating surfaced track
and forest road throughout
Map OS Explorer 348 **Access** no public
transport to the start

**This gentle waymarked walk explores the
southern shore of the Carron Valley
Reservoir. There are toilets at the car
park, and picnic benches and viewpoints
all along the shore path.**

Following a 70 percent drop in annual
rainfall in 1933, Scotland was hit by a
serious drought, raising concerns that
water supplies would run out. To alleviate
future concerns, the Stirlingshire and
Falkirk Water Board began work on the
Carron Valley Reservoir in 1935, damming
the River Carron and building a subsidiary
dam above the River Endrick at the other
end of the valley. Some three miles of
pipes connected the reservoir to the

existing mains supply. The road from
Carronbridge to Fintry was flooded
and a new road built at a higher level.
The total cost was around £230,000; more
than £15m in today's money. The reservoir
was opened in July 1939 by the Secretary
of State for Scotland, John Colville.

It is around 6km long and 2.5km wide,
and holds around 20 billion litres of
water. It was the largest artificial reservoir
in Britain until the Ladybower Reservoir
was built in Derbyshire in 1947.

Today, the reservoir is operated by
Scottish Water. It is a popular walking and
cycling destination. In the summer,
osprey can be seen fishing for brown and
rainbow trout, as well as powan, a rare
freshwater fish which was introduced
from Loch Lomond.

The walk begins in the car park at the
eastern end of the Carron Valley Reservoir,
near the Duncarron Medieval Fort.

◄ Carron Valley Reservoir

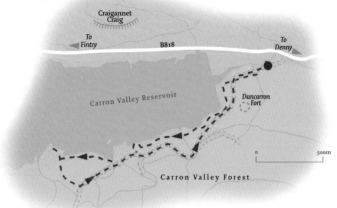

The Clanranald Trust began work on the fort, a replica 12th-century village, in 2008. The following year, the project was gifted a battering ram from the set of the 2010 movie *Robin Hood* by lead actor Russell Crowe, a keen supporter of the Trust. Primarily a visitor attraction, the fort has been used as a location for *Norsemen*, and has supplied weapons, costumes and expertise for *Outlaw King* and *Outlander*.

Walk along the path through the trees, crossing the road and heading towards the dam, following the signs for the Loch Shore Trail.

Approaching the dam, swing around to ascend through the woodland and arrive at a road. Pass above the dam and drop down to meander along close to the reservoir shore.

After 700m or so, head down another surfaced path which leads off towards the shore. Loop around before joining the main path again, meeting almost immediately with a forest road.

Continuing westwards, after crossing a couple of burns, walk down the next path towards the loch shore and follow it to a junction, turning towards the loch again and heading towards a picnic bench on a grassy peninsula that sticks out into the middle of the reservoir. There are excellent views across the loch towards Meikle Bin from the peninsula.

Return to the junction and turn inland, climbing away from the reservoir and heading through a copse of trees to arrive back at the forest road again.

Follow the road back to the car park and the beginning of the walk.

Carron Valley Forest

Distance 13.7km **Time** 3 hours 30
Terrain mostly surfaced forest vehicle
track; damp grassy track to summit of
Black Hill **Map** OS Explorer 348
Access no public transport to the start

**This long but easy walk follows a vehicle
track through the Carron Valley Forest in
the hills to the south of the Carron Valley
Reservoir, climbing to the summit of
Black Hill.**

The forest is the remnant of a blanket
Sitka spruce plantation which began in
the 1940s, reaching its current extent in
the early 1980s. This has now been
restructured, with a mixture of native tree
species and open spaces turning the
plantation into a forest. As well as being
attractive to walkers and cyclists, this is
beneficial to wildlife – look out for red
squirrel and pine marten, and birds such
as osprey and black grouse.

The woodland here is popular with
mountain bikers, and care should be
taken not to stray onto dedicated bike
trails (these are signposted).

Take the path through the trees
from the car park at the eastern end of
the Carron Valley Reservoir, heading
towards the dam and crossing the road.
The path swings uphill as you approach
the dam, emerging onto a forest road.
Turn to pass above the dam, skirting
around a gate. Keep straight on at the
junction before striding uphill at the
next fork.

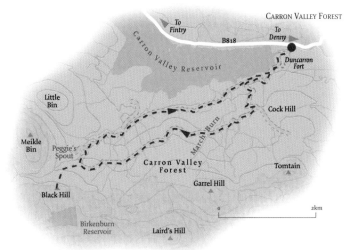

After a couple of switchbacks, turn along a smaller road which leaves the main route, continuing through the forest. Stay on the main path at the next junction to descend slightly before rounding a corner to pass along the edge of a huge clearing.

The road continues uphill, alternating between woodland and felled areas to arrive at a hairpin bend. Here, take the informal track straight ahead that leads up the hill in the shadow of Meikle Bin.

Reaching the end of the track, turn left to cross a couple of dilapidated wooden bridges and saunter up a damp, grassy track to the summit of Black Hill.

The fence at the top of the track stretches eastwards along the Campsie Ridge, and it is possible to follow the fence and the parallel path as far as Tomtain and the Tak-Ma-Doon Road. The actual summit, across the fence

and a few metres west from here, is unmarked. Nevertheless, the view, back across almost the whole of the Carron Valley as far as the dam at the eastern end of the reservoir where the walk started, is impressive.

On the other side of the fence, Birkenburn Reservoir is a few hundred metres away before the hillside drops away towards Kirkintilloch and Cumbernauld. From here, return to the hairpin bend, and strike out downhill. Keep right at the next junction, following signs for the Main Car Park. A burn falls through a deep gorge beside the path and over a waterfall called Peggie's Spout.

Keep straight ahead at the next two junctions, still heading for the Main Car Park. Nearing the reservoir, you can either follow the road or take the more scenic Loch Shore Trail (signposted) to return to the car park.

◄ Carron Valley Forest and Meikle Bin

Tomtain

Distance 3.5km **Time** 1 hour
Terrain grassy hill track, damp underfoot,
even in good weather **Map** OS Explorer 348
Access no public transport to the start

The short straightforward hike up this
453m hill is made even easier by starting
at the Tak-Ma-Doon Road Viewpoint and
Picnic Area, which sits at around 320m
and overlooks Kilsyth. The route is part
of an old drovers' road named the
Campsie Ridge Route, which came
eastwards along the ridge from Black
Hill, crossing Garrel Hill and Tomtain
before dropping down through Denny to
reach the cattle market at Falkirk.

Pleasure is derived not so much from
the fine walk to the summit, but from the
superb 360-degree views across the
Kilsyth Hills and around the eastern and
southern Central Belt.

Turn right out of the Tak-Ma-Doon Road
Viewpoint car park and continue uphill. At
a sign for Kilsyth via Tomtain, turn left,
skirting around a metal barrier to walk
along an obvious grassy track up the hill.

The route climbs gradually upwards,
following a fence, passing conifer trees
and crossing heather-clad hillside in an
almost direct line towards the summit,
which has been visible straight ahead
since the beginning of the walk.

A final short but steep ascent to the top, which is marked by a cairn and a trig point on the other side of the fence, is rewarded with fantastic views straight ahead to Meikle Bin and the Carron Valley Reservoir. The north is dominated by the mountains of the Southern Highlands, and the long, almost vertical escarpment of the Ochil Hills rises beyond Stirling to disappear towards the northeastern horizon. Denny and Falkirk are to the east, stretching out toward Grangemouth Oil Refinery on the shores of the Forth.

Kilsyth sits at the foot of the hill to the south, with the long silvery shard of the Forth & Clyde Canal on its far side.

Just beyond the summit of Tomtain, cairns mark the graves of two chapmen, or pedlars, itinerant traders who would visit households selling various wares or services. According to legend, one killed the other. When the murderer was subsequently tried and executed he was buried beside his victim.

For a longer walk, the path may be followed onwards along the wide ridge of the Kilsyth Hills towards Meikle Bin, but Tomtain offers the finest views. To return, retrace your steps to the car park.

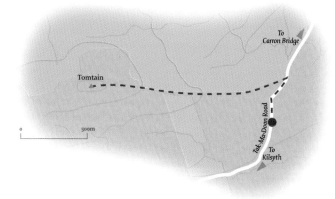

The Colzium Lennox Estate

Distance 3.4km **Time** 1 hour **Terrain** good surfaced and unsurfaced paths; some gentle ascents **Map** OS Explorer 348 **Access** buses to Kilsyth (1km from the start) from Glasgow and Falkirk

This fine walk explores the parkland of an historic estate with lots to discover.

The Colzium Lennox Estate dates to the 12th century, when the Earl of Lennox built a motte and bailey castle on Castle Hill. The estate passed to the Livingstons of Callendar in the 15th century, who built Colzium Castle, an L-plan towerhouse, at the foot of Colzium Glen. The castle was demolished by William Livingstone, 3rd Viscount Kilsyth, in 1703. As he was a Jacobite, Kilsyth forfeited the estate after the 1715 uprising and it passed to the Edmonstones of Duntreath, who built Colzium House in 1783. The estate was acquired by W Mackey Lennox in 1930, who donated it to the people of Kilsyth in 1937.

The walk begins in the car park by the curling pond. To get here, take the first turn-off after entering the estate. Kilsyth is the birthplace of the sport of curling, and this is thought to be the oldest curling pond in the world.

Turn back towards the entrance, but take the first path uphill. Cross a bridge and pass a swing park to arrive at a road. Continue uphill, taking care as the road is used by traffic. Turn uphill again just before a bridge to follow a deep glen through the woodland. The Colzium Burn tumbles over waterfalls in the glen below.

Follow the sign for the Tak-Ma-Doon Road, crossing the burn at an old stone bridge over a waterfall and heading back down the glen again, passing Granny's Mutch, designed as a place to view the glen's waterfalls below – its name comes from its resemblance to a type of bonnet worn by elderly ladies.

Stay by the burn, dropping towards a

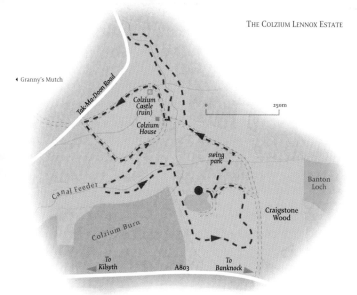

◀ Granny's Mutch

Tak-Ma-Doon Road

Colzium Castle (ruin)

Colzium House

0   250m

swing park

Banton Loch

Canal Feeder

Colzium Burn

Craigstone Wood

To Kilsyth

A803

To Banknock

bridge but, before reaching it, turning back downhill by the burn again. The old icehouse is at the bottom of the hill. Built around 1680, it refrigerated game and eggs, using ice from nearby ponds. It is now home to four species of bat.

Reaching a road, turn right and then right again by Colzium House, heading for the Walled Garden which is well worth exploring. The road swings around to the left, passing a cottage which contains part of the original wall of Colzium Castle. Continue to follow the road as it climbs up the hill.

Just before an exit to Tak-Ma-Doon Road, turn downhill beneath a canopy of trees. Emerging from the trees, turn sharply down the hill, looking down on the memorial to the Battle of Kilsyth

(1645), a victory for the Royalist General James Graham, 1st Marquess of Montrose, over the Covenanter-dominated Scottish Parliament. It was the largest battle fought in Scotland in the Wars of the Three Kingdoms.

Cross Colzium Lade, which feeds Banton Loch and ultimately the Forth & Clyde Canal, and turn left. At a crosspaths, you can cross the lade to the memorial; otherwise, turn down the hill, passing the curling pond and keeping straight ahead at the fork. Bear left at the next fork to enter the Arboretum, with its rare and unusual trees. Continue straight through the Arboretum, turning uphill just before the road. Bear right beyond an old bench to leave the Arboretum, and follow the road back to the curling pond.

Dumbreck Marsh Nature Reserve

Distance 4.8km **Time** 1 hour 15
Terrain an easy walk on good surfaced
paths **Map** OS Explorer 348 **Access** buses
to Kilsyth from Glasgow and Falkirk

Dumbreck Marsh is an important
wetland habitat for a range of animals
and birds. Look out for roe deer and fox.
Common blue damselflies, common
hawker dragonflies, and butterflies such
as orange tips and ringlets flit among
meadowsweet, valerian, ragged robin and
common spotted and northern marsh
orchids. Birdlife includes the shy and
reclusive grasshopper warbler and water
rail, with more success of seeing reed
bunting, sedge warbler and whitethroat.

Despite the peace and quiet, Dumbreck
used to be an industrial area where for
nearly a century coal and coke was
produced. The first shaft was sunk in
1885. In January 1938, nine men suffocated
as the result of a fire in Dumbreck Pit,
including two brothers and their nephew.
The mine closed in the 1960s and, after
being cleared and landscaped, the site was
designated as a nature reserve in 1994.

Cross the road from the Auchinstarry
Quarry car park, and walk along the River
Kelvin Walkway, which begins beside an
ornate old sign welcoming you to Kilsyth.
The track runs parallel to the River Kelvin,
which at this point is little more than a
burn. By the time it reaches Glasgow, and
flows into the Clyde, it will be a wide river.

The walkway follows the line of an old
mineral railway which ran along the
Kelvin. Built in the 1860s, it connected
Dumbreck Pit with the Kelvin Valley
Railway, and was part of a network of such
lines which joined the Kilsyth area's
numerous mines, quarries and gravel

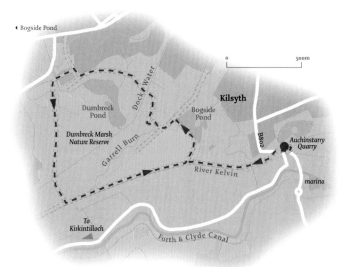

workings. It remained in use until the closure of the pit.

Walk past a large grassy meadow, and turn away from the riverside at the next junction. Continue across a wooden walkway with excellent views across Bogside Pond to the distant Kilsyth Burns & Old Parish Church. Teal, heron, pochard and swan can often be seen on the pond.

Reaching the Garrell Burn, turn left to stroll alongside the burn. Turn right at the first junction, bearing right again almost immediately to cross the burn at a bridge. The burn was rerouted in early 2022 to help conserve the local wetland habitat. As a result, by July 2022, salmon were present in the Garrell Burn for the first time in 100 years.

Bear left beyond the bridge, heading left again at the next junction. After crossing a couple of bridges, continue straight ahead at a junction, bearing right as you pass the rear of some houses, then immediately left to meander across a pond on a boardwalk. Keep right where the boardwalk forks.

Arriving back on dry land, turn left to climb gradually uphill and cross a wide open meadow. The hill to the left of the path is the remains of a coal bing, the only reminder of the area's history. Crossing a metal bridge, Castle Hill, with its white trig point on the summit, can be seen straight ahead.

Arriving quickly back by the River Kelvin, turn left to walk back to the start.

Croy Hill and the Antonine Wall

Distance 10.5km **Time** 2 hours 45
Terrain canal towpath; hill tracks
Map OS Explorer 348 **Access** buses to
Kilsyth from Glasgow and Falkirk

**Separated by almost two millennia,
the Forth & Clyde Canal and the Antonine
Wall run in parallel across the narrow
waist of Scotland. This route follows the
canal before charting the route of the
wall back along a ridge.**

The route begins at the car park at
Auchinstarry Quarry, which at one time
produced whinstone setts to pave the
streets of Glasgow. Turn left out of the
car park to follow the road around to the
canal. Drop down to walk west along
the towpath.

First proposed in around 1710, the
Forth & Clyde Canal is the oldest
surviving canal in Scotland. Construction
began in 1768, and took 22 years to
complete. It closed in 1963, but was
redeveloped for leisure activities as part
of the Millennium Link Project.

After 2.6km, cross the canal at the lifting
bridge which carries the road to Twechar.
The bridge was built in 1960, just before
the canal closed, allowing Twechar to be
reached by a bus service for the first time.
The remains of a railway bridge, which
connected the coalmines north of the
canal to the main Edinburgh to Glasgow
line, can be seen a few metres west.

Beyond the war memorial, take the
track signposted for Bar Hill Fort, going
through a gate and bearing right. Pass
through another couple of gates,
following the John Muir Way to the ruins
of the fort. Constructed in 142AD, the
Antonine Wall marked the northern
frontier of the Roman Empire. The fort

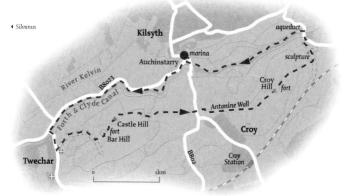

◄ Silvanus

Kilsyth

marina

Auchinstarry

aqueduct

sculpture

Croy Hill fort

River Kelvin

B8023

Forth & Clyde Canal

Antonine Wall

Castle Hill fort
Bar Hill

Croy

B802

Twechar

Croy Station

0   1km

on Bar Hill was one of 17 known forts built along the course of the wall (although it is actually just south of the wall) and would have been home to around 500 men. The bathhouse gives a wonderful insight into the lives of the soldiers and would have been one of the most important buildings on the site. Continue along the John Muir Way, following a broken-down drystane dyke before climbing steeply to the summit of Castle Hill, which is marked with a trig point.

Keep following the John Muir Way to drop down and turn onto a formal path, descending through the trees and two more gates. The path becomes a narrow country road, which drops down towards Croy. Cross the B802 and go through the gate opposite to follow a dirt track across a pasture. Reaching a road, skirt around the barrier and immediately turn left along a long straight track.

Where the road curves to the right, continue straight ahead through a gate,

signposted for Croy Hill. Begin to climb, bearing left and left again to reach the summit, which commands superb views across Kilsyth and the Kilsyth Hills.

Drop down from the hill, still following the John Muir Way. Meeting a surfaced path, follow it downhill to a huge sculpture of a Roman head. The sculpture, designed by artist Svetlana Kondakova and named *Silvanus* after the Roman god of the woods, looks out from the line of the Antonine Wall towards what the Romans considered barbarian territory.

Bear right beyond the head to descend to the canal. The grand but derelict building on the hillside opposite is the Craigmarloch Stables, where horses that operated this part of the canal were kept. Cross the canal, and drop down to follow the towpath west. In the 18th and 19th centuries, Auchinstarry Basin was where coal from Kilsyth was loaded onto canal boats and taken to Glasgow. Leave the towpath just beyond the marina, and follow the road back to the car park.

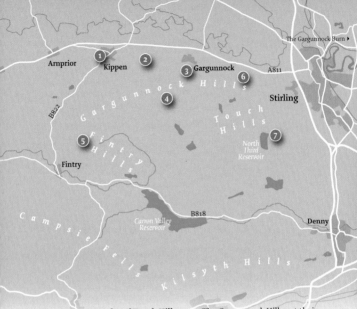

The Fintry, Gargunnock and Touch Hills form the spectacular northeastern edge of the Campsies, where a 13km-long basalt escarpment towers over the Carse of Stirling. Here, the infant River Forth meanders towards Stirling against the impressive backdrop of the mountains of the Southern Highlands.

According to an early tourist guide, the Fintry Hills were once inhabited by a race of Fingalian heroes. The name came, it claimed, from *Fean*, 'a giant', and *tre*, 'a country' – literally 'Land of the Giants'.

More likely, its source was the Brittonic *fin*, meaning 'boundary'. The Fintry Hills form the watershed between the Forth and the Clyde, and were also the border of the Kingdom of Strathclyde.

The Gargunnock Hills get their name from the village of Gargunnock, which sits below the escarpment. The village derives its name from the Gaelic *garbh chuinneag*, meaning 'a rough or uneven pool'.

Perhaps the first problem that walkers will have with the Touch Hills is how to pronounce their name. Pronounced *Took*, it derives from the Gaelic *tulach*, meaning 'hillock', and is first recorded in 1329 as Tulch. The Touch Estate, situated beneath Scout Head, was acquired by Alexander Seton in the 15th century. His descendant, Elizabeth Seton, was a supporter of the Jacobites, and played host to Bonnie Prince Charlie at Touch House a week before the Battle of Prestonpans.

The Fintry, Gargunnock and Touch Hills

Kippen circular

Distance 6.1km **Time** 1 hour 45
Terrain well-defined surfaced and
unsurfaced tracks and roads
Map OS Explorer 366 **Access** buses to
Kippen from Glasgow and Stirling

**This pleasing rural ramble commands
excellent views across Flanders Moss
and the Carse of Stirling towards the
Southern Highlands.**

The route begins by the war memorial
at the foot of Kippen's Main Street. Walk
down Rennie's Loan, an attractive cobbled
lane to the right of the memorial. The
Rennies were blacksmiths here for six
generations until The Smiddy was gifted
to the National Trust for Scotland in 1982
by Andrew Rennie.

The lane soon becomes an unsurfaced
track which quickly leaves the village,
continuing straight ahead at a junction.
Emerge briefly onto tarmac, heading

straight on through a gate and along
another unsurfaced track which descends
to meet with a road close to the A811.
Turn uphill, passing a farm and rising to
meet with the B8037.

Turn left and walk up the roadside path
for a little before crossing to follow the
public footpath to Broich and Fintry Road
(signposted). This climbs the driveway to
Arngomery House gently uphill. Bear left
where the road drops down to Arngomery
House, built in 1812.

Beyond a gate, wander along the edge of
a pasture to another gate into woodland
on the opposite side. This track is part of
the Broich and Arnmanuel peat road,
which was used to transport peat cut
from the Carse of Stirling.

Walk through the woodland, where the
Broich Burn tumbles over little waterfalls
in the gorge below. The track soon
becomes a very minor road, which rises to

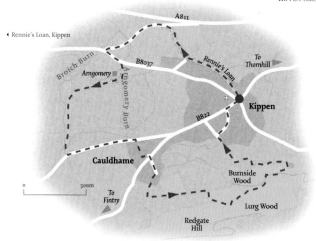

◀ Rennie's Loan, Kippen

a junction. Turn uphill and head back towards Kippen. As you reach the edge of the village, turn along a hedge-lined gravel track that leads off between the houses. At the far end, walk up the road opposite, bearing right along a track where the road stops.

Forth Vineyards was established here in 1891, and by 1922 was home to the Kippen Vine, the world's largest. It produced over a tonne of grapes annually, which were sold as a luxury food in stores across Britain. The vine was destroyed in 1964 when a buyer could not be found for the vineyard.

Following the public footpath, skirt around the gate at the top of the hill and go straight on through another gate to border some woodland for a little before keeping right at a wooden gate to head uphill on a gravel track.

Reaching a road, continue up the hill to a junction. Follow the sign towards Kippen into the trees of Burnside Wood, bearing right along a woodland track to descend gradually. In 2008, a National Lottery award was used to finance the regeneration of Burnside Wood. Native trees replaced non-native species and these woodland tracks were created to allow access and support environmental education activities.

Cross some marshland by a boardwalk, swinging right by a bench and heading downhill to another boardwalk which skirts around a pond. Turn left onto a surfaced track, following it across a bridge and around the edge of a football pitch.

Turn back towards Kippen at the junction, following Castlehill Loan to the Main Street and heading downhill to return to the beginning of the walk.

The Old Military Road

Distance **12.1km** Time **3 hours 15**
Terrain **good surfaced and unsurfaced
tracks and roads throughout**
Map **OS Explorer 348** Access **buses to
Kippen from Glasgow and Stirling**

Although known as a military road,
this route between Stirling and
Dumbarton had been in use long before
the Jacobite uprisings which prompted
the road network. By the time the
military rebuilt the road, between 1770
and 1784, the Jacobite threat was waning.
It was handed over to the local county
in 1790. This route follows the old road
from Kippen to Gargunnock, returning
via a pleasant tree-lined passage.

Take the road that leads off directly
opposite the war memorial at the bottom
end of Kippen's Main Street. Leaving the
village, the road quickly becomes a

country lane which terminates at the
hamlet of Glentirranmuir, but continue
down the track at the far end, where a gate
leads into a grassy pasture. The hill to the
right, known as Brokencastle, was the site
of an ancient fort.

Cross the pasture and head into a
shallow gully, rounding a corner to swing
down over Boquhan Bridge. After a while,
briefly join a country road, passing an
ornate red sandstone building. Keep
straight on to emerge onto open hillside
where the view north is dominated by the
huge pyramid of Ben Ledi.

Pass a farm and go straight over a
crossroads, where an old sign points to
Gargunnock in two directions. According
to local legend, the bridge at this spot was
the scene of a fatal carriage accident.
A ghostly coach and horses are reputed
to re-enact their final journey here.

◀ The Old Military Road

Go through a gate to follow a woodland track along the side of a fence. This is the Leckie Estate, formerly home to the Youngers' home until the Second World War, when it became a military hospital. Today, it has been converted into luxury apartments.

Drop down to join the main drive to the house, keeping right and right again to follow a road through the trees. Descend through a pair of iron gates, passing a farm to join a country road which leads into Gargunnock. In the centre of Gargunnock, turn sharply right by a memorial drinking fountain to cross the

Gargunnock Burn (there is a footbridge beside the old bridge) and head up Main Street. After 300m, turn onto Stevenson Street and take the track between the houses at the top end. Cross a road, keeping straight on through a staggered gatepost and walking into the countryside along a tree-lined track known as The Beeches.

At the end of the track, keep straight on along a narrow road, passing a sign for Knock O'Ronald. Immediately beyond an old stone bridge over the Leckie Burn, turn right to follow the burn back to the crossroads and the double Gargunnock signpost, and trace the outward route back to Kippen.

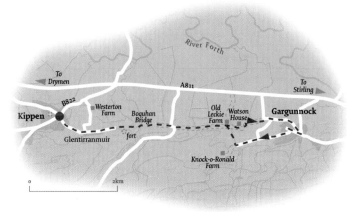

Downie's Loup

Distance 4.3km **Time** 1 hour 15
Terrain surfaced vehicle track; steep
grassy hill track **Map** OS Explorer 348
Access buses to Gargunnock from
Glasgow and Stirling

**This short walk leads from Gargunnock
to Downie's Loup, a fine hidden
waterfall which cascades down the
basalt escarpment of Carleatheran.**

The walk begins outside the
Gargunnock Inn, on Gargunnock's Main
Street. Head down the hill, crossing an
iron footbridge beside the old roadbridge.
The footbridge was installed in 1975, but
was built using parts salvaged from an
1826 footbridge over the Kelty Water at
Gartmore, near Aberfoyle. The roadbridge
beside it dates from 1775. This is the first
of three times that this route crosses the
Gargunnock Burn. At one time, the burn
turned one cornmill and one flourmill on

its short journey to join the River Forth
a little north of the village.

Keep straight on to head up Manse
Brae, passing the 1774 Parish Church and
crossing Moray Place before turning
uphill onto a wide aggregate vehicle
track as you leave the village.

Go through a series of four gates,
winding gradually uphill to reach a
junction. Bear left, curling almost
immediately up the hill. The vehicle
track soon peters out and is replaced
with a wide gorse-lined grassy track
which heads directly up to a stile in the
corner of a pasture by a disused quarry.

Cross the stile, turning right to climb
diagonally uphill to the opposite corner of
the pasture, where a thick iron sheet
covers an old well. Water can be heard
from below. Pass the well and walk along
a short rocky track which leads across the
top end of a gorse-filled gorge. Suddenly,

◀ Downie's Loup

Gargunnock

To A811

Thompson's
Wood

Gargunnock Burn

Johnstone's
Wood

Millershill
Wood

Dinnin
Wood

Gilboa
Wood

0   500m

Downie's
Loup

the waterfall comes into view just a few metres away.

Downie's Loup is the lowest of three large waterfalls which carry the Gargunnock Burn down from Carleatheran. Downie was a member of a local family, who seems to have made a daredevil sport of jumping the falls on his horse. He was killed on his third jump.

Old maps place Downie's Loup at a lower and smaller waterfall, around 50m downstream, but the name has come to be attributed to the higher and more dramatic 12m perpendicular fall here.

You can bear left for a close-up of the waterfall, but the main route keeps right to descend a short but steep track into the gorge. Duck beneath a thick branch that has arched across from a tree on the opposite bank to embed itself in the wall of the gorge. If the burn is in spate, it would be prudent to turn back here, but

otherwise, step carefully across and follow the track up the other side of the gorge.

Climb over the wooden fence a few metres beyond the top, and wander down a grassy track, following the line of a fence to meet with a gate across a surfaced vehicle track.

Turn right onto the vehicle track, continuing along it to cross the Gargunnock Burn for the third and final time, before meeting with the outward route and returning to Gargunnock.

87

Carleatheran

Distance 14.4km **Time** 3 hours 45
Terrain surfaced vehicle track; grassy hill
track, boggy in places **Map** OS Explorer
348 **Access** buses to Gargunnock from
Glasgow and Stirling

The massive escarpment of Carleatheran
may look a daunting prospect from
below, but the vehicle track that twists
effortlessly up the crags makes this an
uncomplicated yet rewarding hike. The
hill's name is derived from the Brythonic
Caer Latheron, meaning 'Fort by the Mire',
and the summit is indeed boggy in places.

The route begins by the church on
Manse Brae in Gargunnock. Head uphill
out of the village, turning up a concrete
track towards Hillhead Farm (signposted)
as the road descends. Skirt to the right of
the farm buildings before crossing the
farmyard (be aware this is a working
farm). Exit through the gate, turning
uphill through another gate, where the
track continues along the edge of a field.

After going through another gate, wind
your way up the hill, initially on a wide
ledge beneath a series of high crags. As it
climbs, the track becomes wider and, in
the late spring, the air hangs heavy with
the coconut aroma of the gorse bushes.
As you climb, the view begins to open out
towards Stirling Castle, the Wallace
Monument and the Ochil Hills. Down
below, the River Forth can be seen
meandering across the Carse of Stirling.

Despite climbing a relatively steep part
of the hillside, the incline is gradual,
ascending in a series of long switchbacks
before levelling out at the top to stride
along the hillside, and climbing very
gradually before veering uphill again to
pass an attractive wooden hut.

Leave the vehicle track opposite a
couple of large metal storage sheds to
climb uphill again on a grassy ATV track,
bearing right where the track splits to
head beneath a small crag.

The ground becomes boggy underfoot

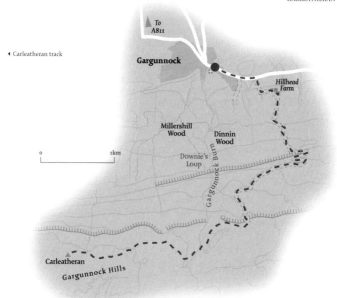

◀ Carleatheran track

To
A811

Gargunnock

Hillhead
Farm

Millershill
Wood

Dinnin
Wood

Downie's
Loup

Gargunnock Burn

0   1km

Carleatheran
Gargunnock Hills

as you approach the Gargunnock Burn. Hop over the burn and walk parallel to it for a little before climbing away from it across the open hillside again. This moorland plateau is home to birds such as red and black grouse, curlew, lapwing, golden plover, snipe, hen harrier, merlin and golden eagles. Look out for mammals such as deer and mountain hares too.

Bear right around a grassy hillock, crossing a makeshift bridge and going through a gate in an old drystane dyke. As the ATV track continues westwards, the cairn at the summit comes into view. The final ascent to the cairn is steep but short. It sits on top of a large mound

which, some have speculated, is an overgrown broch – accounting for the fort in the hill's name.

From the cairn, a trig point surrounded by modern stone shelters, there are excellent views across Stirling to the castle and the Wallace Monument on top of Abbey Craig, set against the dramatic backdrop of Dumyat and the Ochil Hills.

The huge turbines of the Kingsburn Windfarm are to the south. Opened in 2016, these generate enough green energy to power 17,800 homes. Loch Lomond can be seen in the distance to the west.

Having admired the view from the summit, retrace your steps to the start.

Stronend

Distance 13km **Time** 3 hours 30
Terrain good track for the initial gradual
climb, followed by damp grassy track
across moorland to the summit
Map OS Explorer 348 **Access** no public
transport to the start

**The sometimes damp underfoot climb
to the summit of Stronend is rewarded
with spectacular views across the Forth
Valley from Stirling to Loch Lomond.**

At 511m, Stronend is the highest of the
Fintry Hills, standing sentinel at the far
end of the spectacular escarpment that
stretches southwestwards from Stirling
for some 12km.

To get to the start point leave the A811
1km east of Boquhan, following the sign
for Glinns Road. After around 800m, turn
left, then immediately right, following the
single-track road for 3.7km to reach a wide
lay-by by Bailie Bow's Bridge, with room
for around four vehicles.

Walk back along the road, turning uphill
across a cattle grid at the entrance to
Ballochleam Farm to follow a vehicle
track. Ignoring the road down to the
farmhouse, continue through another
two gates and walk quickly up the pass
between Stronend and Carleatheran,
bringing a magnificent panorama of the
Highland Boundary into view.

Approaching the top of the hill the
Spout of Ballochleam, where the Boquhan
Burn crashes dramatically into the gully
between the two hills, is an impressive
sight when the burn is in spate.

Beyond another gate, you arrive on the
open heather moorland that stretches
across the long flat plateau of both
Stronend and Carleatheran. Here, an
obvious grassy track leaves the main path
through a very basic wooden gate on the
right to strike out towards Stronend.

Drop briefly to cross the Boquhan Burn
before climbing the short but steep

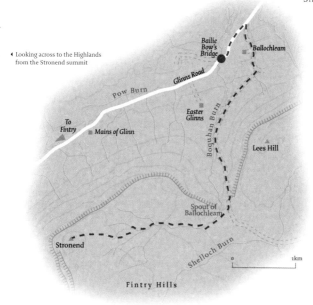

◀ Looking across to the Highlands from the Stronend summit

embankment on the other side. Turn left at the top and follow the grassy track above the burn, climbing gradually across the open heather moorland, with its vegetation of heather, grasses, berries and mosses. This is a globally rare habitat. The majority of the world's heather moorland resources are found in Scotland. The peaty soil beneath the surface acts as a carbon sink and plays an important role in controlling climate change.

Soon the track levels out again to cross a number of narrow burns, mostly at bridges built out of old railway sleepers, but you have to step across a few of them,

making a beeline for the summit. Despite the relatively flat and featureless moorland, the track climbs sharply uphill past a large boulder, which can be seen on the horizon from the approach, to reach the summit. The hilltop, marked by a trig point sitting within a shepherd's shelter cairn, appears quite suddenly.

The summit of Stronend offers fantastic views as far as Loch Lomond, Conic Hill and Ben Lomond. Further east, the Lake of Menteith sits in the foreground, in front of Ben Ledi and the other hills of the Trossachs.

There is no easy way back to the start point other than to retrace your steps.

Garshellach Forest

Distance 6.4km **Time** 1 hour 45
Terrain good vehicle track; forest track
for the final 400m **Map** OS Explorer 348
Access no public transport to the start

Sitting at the very northeastern edge of
the Campsies, Scout Head, sometimes
erroneously called Scout Hill, rises
sharply out of the Carse of Stirling,
marking the beginning of the range of
hills which stretches all the way to
Dumgoyne by Killearn.

This leisurely and unchallenging walk
follows a wide vehicle track up the
wooded slopes, skirting the summit to
reach a grassy knoll. Higher up, the views
are limited, but the initial climb offers a
superb panorama across the Carse of
Stirling to the Highlands and the Ochils.

The route begins at a rough lay-by 400m
along Touch Road from its junction with

the A811, signposted for Cambusbarron.
A wide vehicle track leads up the hill
opposite the lay-by.

Skirt around a metal barrier, passing a
sign for Garshellach Forest. As you climb,
Stirling Castle can be seen prominently
on its rocky crag behind you. The Wallace
Monument sits in front of Dumyat, and
the long escarpment of the Ochil Hills
stretches westwards into the distance.
To the north, the narrow ribbon of the
River Forth snakes across the flat plains of
the Carse of Stirling, while the Highland
Boundary Fault and the prominent
Munros of the Southern Highlands can be
seen beyond. On a clear day, you can see
as far as Arthur's Seat in Edinburgh.

The views are soon lost as the track
disappears into the trees. Keep an eye out
for red deer, red squirrel, and the ever-
elusive pine marten. Turn uphill at a fork,

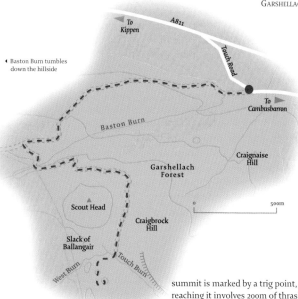

◀ Baston Burn tumbles down the hillside

summit is marked by a trig point, but reaching it involves 200m of thrashing through the undergrowth from here and offers no views.

Swing to the south to continue to skirt around the summit, dropping down briefly to cross a bridge high over the West Burn, which plummets over a delightful waterfall a little upstream.

The vehicle track terminates suddenly beyond the bridge, but walk up the narrow foot track which leads gently up the hill, curling around to a fork. The track to the right quickly becomes boggy and eventually peters out altogether, so bear left, climbing to reach a rounded knowe surrounded by trees.

This is a good spot for a picnic, before returning to the beginning of the walk.

continuing to climb through a couple of zigzags before straightening out.

Soon the track, lined with occasional gorse bushes, doubles back on itself to climb through a forest of Scots pines. At another switchback, the picturesque Baston Burn is routed beneath the track before tumbling down the hill through the trees.

Just before the track turns sharply uphill again, a deep gorge known as Shallow Tongue drops away to the left. Continue up the hill through a couple more switchbacks before straightening out to head eastwards beneath the wooded summit of Scout Head. The

93

North Third Reservoir

Distance 9.3km **Time** 2 hours 30
Terrain formal and informal hillside and
woodland tracks; some steep ascents.
Sauchie Craig is not suitable for dogs or
small children **Map** OS Explorer 348
Access no public transport to the start

**Where this walk scores is in the sheer
variety of landscapes it passes through,
from high crags to reservoir to woodland
and riverside.**

The route begins on the unnumbered
minor road to the south of North Third
Reservoir, where there is a small number
of parking spaces 270m or so uphill from
the bridge over the Bannock Burn. Walk
down the hill, turning right to follow the
burn towards the reservoir immediately
after the bridge.

The reservoir, built in 1911 to supply
water to Grangemouth, dams the Bannock
Burn. The dam has been raised twice, in

1934 and in 1936. Wander along the shore,
crossing several bridges, to reach and
cross the dam at the far end.

At the end of the dam, bear left,
following a waymark post through a
firebreak in the forest. The track through
the firebreak soon becomes a vehicle track
which climbs gently back up the hill
again. Turn off left at a cairn by the side of
the path, following a woodland track
which undulates gently through a forest
of conifers and silver birch. Eventually,
drop into the gorge to follow the Bannock
Burn through the trees.

Keep left to continue along the
riverbank, passing the ruins of the
Craigends Lime Kilns, dating from the
18th century. Here, rock quarried from
Sauchie Craig was heated to produce lime
for agricultural use.

At a T-junction by a rudimentary
concrete bridge, follow the road briefly

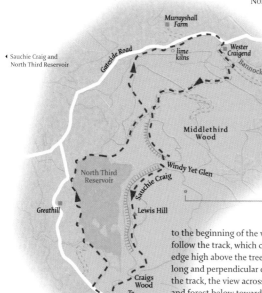

◄ Sauchie Craig and
North Third Reservoir

Murrayshall
Farm

lime
kilns

Wester
Craigend

Bannock Burn

Gateside Road

Middlethird
Wood

North Third
Reservoir

Windy Yet Glen

Sauchie Craig

Greathill

Lewis Hill

0   1km

Craigs
Wood
To
Stirling

into the trees (right) before swinging sharply left to walk along the edge of the forest for a little. Turn uphill past a gate, then left to begin a long steep climb.

Looking back, you can see along the Ochils escarpment to The Law and King's Seat. Arthur's Seat can be seen on the horizon and the Pentlands to the southeast. Continue straight ahead at a junction, crossing a wide turning circle. As the road descends, a track disappears up the hill into the trees.

If you want to avoid the steep drops of Sauchie Craig, continue along the road to rejoin the outward route, following it back to the beginning of the walk. Otherwise, follow the track, which climbs to a cliff edge high above the trees. Despite the long and perpendicular drop right beside the track, the view across the reservoir and forest below towards the distant Highlands is superb.

After a while, the path veers away from the crags to descend through the woods. At a junction, turn left to climb a series of switchbacks which cling to the side of Lewis Hill. Levelling out, amble through the heather towards the distinctive white trig point which marks the 266m-high summit. This is a great vantage point on a clear day, with views all around to Ben Ledi, Stuc a'Chroin, Ben Vorlich, Ben Chonzie, the Ochils, the Lomond Hills, the Forth Bridges, the Pentland Hills and Meikle Bin.

Continue along the track to drop down the hill and back to the beginning of the walk.

Index